PERSPECTIVES IN SOCIAL INQUIRY

PERSPECTIVES IN SOCIAL INQUIRY

CLASSICS, STAPLES AND PRECURSORS IN SOCIOLOGY

Advisory Editors

ROBERT K. MERTON
ARON HALBERSTAM

SOCIAL LAWS

G[abriel] de Tarde

ARNO PRESS

A New York Times Company

New York — 1974

Reprint Edition 1974 by Arno Press Inc.

Reprinted from a copy in
  The University of Illinois Library

PERSPECTIVES IN SOCIAL INQUIRY
ISBN for complete set: 0-405-05490-4
See last pages of this volume for titles.

Manufactured in the United States of America

————◆————

Library of Congress Cataloging in Publication Data

Tarde, Gabriel de, 1843-1904.
   Social laws: an outline of sociology.

   (Perspectives in social inquiry)
   Reprint of the ed. published by Macmillan, New York.
   Translation of Les lois sociales, esquisse d'une
sociologie.
   1. Sociology. I. Title. II. Series.
HM201.T413 1974   301   73-14183
ISBN 0-405-05527-7

SOCIAL LAWS

AN OUTLINE OF SOCIOLOGY

SOCIAL LAWS

AN OUTLINE OF SOCIOLOGY

BY

G. TARDE

TRANSLATED FROM THE FRENCH

BY

HOWARD C. WARREN
ASSISTANT PROFESSOR OF EXPERIMENTAL PSYCHOLOGY
IN PRINCETON UNIVERSITY

WITH A PREFACE BY

JAMES MARK BALDWIN

New York

THE MACMILLAN COMPANY

LONDON: MACMILLAN & CO., LTD.

1899

Norwood Press

J. S. Cushing & Co. — Berwick & Smith

Norwood Mass. U.S.A.

CONTENTS

EDITOR'S PREFACE

IT goes without saying that no introduction of M. Tarde is necessary to
English and American readers who are
versed in current sociological discussions.
To the general reader, therefore, and to
him alone, I venture, on the insistent
request of the publishers, to say that in
this little book he will find the leading
ideas of one of the most authoritative
and distinguished living writers in sociology and social psychology. M. Tarde's
larger works are summarized and his
system shown to be a system in these
pages — in a way that he humorously
describes in his preface. In fulfilling the
purpose of systematization, however, the
book makes a contribution to the theory
of science at the same time that it ex-

hibits a way of treating sociological data under certain general laws. Whether or no these laws — " repetition, opposition, adaptation " — be established in the form proposed by the author, at any rate they are likely to be much discussed and to take rank as brilliant formulations in the development of a branch of knowledge in which synthesis and constructive hypothesis are sorely needed.

Readers of this little volume will certainly turn to M. Tarde's larger books, and it is interesting to know that a translation of his remarkable work, *Les Lois de l'Imitation*, is under the favorable consideration of one of the leading American publishing houses.

I may add that the fine quality of Professor Warren's translation has made the " editorial" function a piece of pleasant form.

J. MARK BALDWIN.

PRINCETON,
    July, 1899.

PREFACE

In this little volume, which contains the substance of some lectures delivered at the *Collége libre des sciences sociales*, in October, 1897, I aim to give, not a mere outline or *résumé* of my three principal works on general Sociology,[1] but rather the internal bond that unites them. Their real connection, which has possibly escaped the reader's notice, is here made evident through arguments of a more general character, which enable us, I think, to embrace within a single point of view these three parts, published separately, of a common thought — these *disjecta membra*, as it were, of a single

[1] *Les Lois de l'Imitation* (The Laws of Imitation), *L'Opposition universelle* (Universal Opposition), and *La Logique sociale* (Social Logic).

body of ideas. I may possibly be told that it would have been quite as well had I first presented as a systematic whole that which I have actually cut up into three separate publications. But, aside from the fact that a work in several volumes is apt (and with reason) to alarm the modern reader, why should we wear ourselves out in the work of building up such great structures — such complete edifices? Since our successors will have nothing more pressing to do than demolish these structures in order to make some other use of the materials or take possession of a detached wing, it is surely as well to spare them the task of demolition, by delivering our thought in fragments only. At the same time, for the sake of those few who take the same pleasure in putting together what is offered them in fragments, that others do in tearing down what is presented to them in completed form, it is perhaps not altogether bootless to add to the scattered parts of one's work a sketch or outline, indicating the general plan which the author would like to have carried out had he possessed the requisite strength and boldness. This is the only excuse offered for this little volume.

April, 1898. G. T.

SOCIAL LAWS

INTRODUCTION

WHEN we traverse the gallery of history, and observe its motley succession of fantastic paintings — when we examine in a cursory way the successive races of mankind, all different and constantly changing, our first impression is apt to be that the phenomena of social life are incapable of any general expression or scientific law, and that the attempt to found a system of sociology is wholly chimerical. But the first herdsmen who scanned the starry heavens, and the first tillers of the soil who essayed to discover the secrets of plant life, must have been impressed in much the same way by the sparkling disorder of the firmament, with its manifold meteors, as well as by the exuberant diversity of vegetable and animal forms. The idea of explaining sky or forest by a small number of logically concatenated notions, under the name of astronomy or biology, had it occurred to them, would have appeared in their eyes the height of extravagance. And there is no less complexity — no less real irregularity and apparent caprice — in the world of meteors and in the interior of the virgin forest, than in the recesses of human history.

How is it, then, that in spite of this changing diversity in the domain of sky and forest, among physical objects and living beings, we have seen the birth and gradual growth of the sciences of physics and biology? There are three essential elements involved in the development of these branches, and these must be carefully distinguished before we can form a complete and exact notion of what is meant by a certain noun and adjective that are very widely used, namely, *science* and *scientific*.

In the first place, then, men began to perceive some similarities in the midst of these differences, some *repetitions* among these variations. Such are the periodic return of the same conditions of the heavens, the cycle of the seasons, the regularly repeated succession of ages among living creatures,— youth, maturity, and old age, — and the traits common to individuals of the same species. There is no science of the individual as such ; all science is general; that is, it considers the individual as repeated, or as capable of indefinite repetition.

Science is the coördination of phenomena regarded from the side of their *repetitions*. But this does not mean that differentiation is not an essential mode of procedure for the scientific mind. It is the duty of science to differentiate, as well as to assimilate ; but only to the extent that the object differentiated is a *type* in nature yielding a certain number of copies, and capable of indefinite reproduction. A specific type may be discovered and carefully defined; but, if it be found to belong to a single individual only, and to be incapable of transmission to posterity, it fails to interest the scientist, except as a curious monstrosity. Repetition means the production of something that at the same time preserves the original; it implies simple and elementary causation without creation. The effect reproduces the cause point by point, just as in the case of transmission of movement from one body to another, or the transmission of life from a living being to its progeny.

But in addition to the question of *reproduction*, the phenomena involved in *destruction* are of interest to science. And hence, in every sphere of fact to which she directs her attention, science must endeavor to discover, in the second place, the *oppositions* that exist there and are germane to her object. Thus, she must con-

sider the equilibrium of forces, the symmetry of forms, the struggles of living organisms, and the strife among all creatures.

But this is not all, nor even the most
important element. The *adaptations* of
phenomena, and their relations in creative production, must above all be dealt
with. The scientist labors continually to
detect, disentangle, and explain these
harmonies. With their discovery, he succeeds in establishing a higher adaptation,
namely, the harmony of his system of notions and hypotheses with the interrelations of facts.

Thus science consists in viewing any
fact whatsoever under three aspects, corresponding, respectively, to the repetitions,
oppositions, and adaptations which it contains, and which are obscured by a mass
of variations, dissymmetries, and disharmonies. The relation of cause to effect,
in fact, is not the only element which properly constitutes scientific knowledge. If
it were so, pragmatic history, the mere

concatenation of causes and effects, which simply teaches that certain battles and certain insurrections had such and such consequences, would be the most perfect example of science. Yet history, as we know, becomes a science only when the relations of causality which it reveals are shown to exist between a general cause, capable of repetition or actually repeating itself, and a general effect, also repeated or capable of repetition.

Again, mathematics never reveals causality in operation. When a cause is postulated under the name of *function*, it is always disguised as an equation. Yet mathematics is certainly a science; in fact, it is the prototype of all science. And why? Because nowhere has a more complete elimination of the dissimilar and individual side of phenomena been effected, and nowhere do they present a more exact and definite repetition, and a more symmetrical opposition. The great fault of mathematics lies in its not perceiving, or taking

adequately into account, the adaptations
of phenomena. Hence arises that insufficiency of the science, so strongly felt by
philosophers, especially the geometricians
among them, such as Descartes, Comte,
and Cournot.

Repetition, opposition, and adaptation,
I repeat, are the three keys which science
employs to open up the arcana of the universe. She seeks, before all else, not the
mere causes, but the laws that govern the
repetition, opposition, and adaptation of
phenomena. These are three different
species of laws, which must certainly not
be confounded; yet they are quite as
closely connected as they are distinct. In
biology, for example, the tendency of species to multiply in geometric progression
(a law of repetition) forms the basis of the
struggle for existence and natural selection
(a law of opposition); and the appearance
of individual variations, the production of
various individual aptitudes and harmonies,
and the correlation of parts in growth

(laws of adaptation) are necessary to the proper functioning of both.[1]

But, of these three keys, the first and third are far more important than the second. The first is the great pass-key; while the third, of finer construction, gives access to treasures deeply hidden and most precious. The second, an intermediary, of lesser importance, reveals certain strifes and collisions of temporary utility, which are destined to fade away little by little, though never completely, even this partial disappearance being effected only after numerous transformations and attenuations.

These reflections were needed in order to show what sociology must be, if it is

[1] It will be noted that Cuvier and the naturalists of his time, including even his opponent Lamarck, sought out primarily the laws of adaptation, while, on the other hand, Darwin and his evolutionist disciples preferred to consider the phenomena of life from the standpoint of repetitions and oppositions (the Malthusian law and the law of the struggle for existence), though they certainly took into account organic adaptation also, which is the most important fact of all.

to deserve the name of science, and along what paths sociologists must guide its course, if they wish to see it assume, unchallenged, its proper rank. Like every other science, it will attain this only when it has gained, and is conscious of possessing, its own domain of repetitions, its own domain of oppositions, and its own domain of adaptations, each characteristic of itself and belonging wholly to itself. Sociology can only make progress when it succeeds in substituting true repetitions, oppositions, and harmonies for false ones, as all the other sciences have done before it. And in place of repetitions, oppositions, and adaptations that are true but vague, it must find others that become ever more exact as it advances.

Let us place ourselves at each of these standpoints in turn, first of all to ascertain whether or not the evolution of science in general, and sociology in particular, has taken place in the manner which I have already imperfectly defined, and which I shall be able to define more fully as we proceed; in the second place, to point out the laws of social development under each of these three aspects.

CHAPTER I

THE REPETITION OF PHENOMENA

IMAGINE ourselves in the presence of some great object, such as the starry sky, the sea, a forest, a crowd, or a city. From every part of such an object emanate impressions which strike the senses of the savage as well as those of the scientist; but to the latter these manifold and incoherent sensations suggest certain logically correlated notions, which together make up a bundle of explanatory principles. How has this gradual elaboration of mere sensations into notions and laws come about? By what process has our knowledge of such phenomena become more and more scientific? The change, I contend, has come about, in the first place, because we have been constantly discovering a greater number of resemblances among these phenomena, and because, in place of the merely superficial, apparent, and deceptive resemblances among them, we have come to discern certain other resemblances, at once deeper and more real. In fact, we have passed from complex and confused resemblances and repetitions of the whole to resemblances and repetitions of the parts. These latter are more difficult to discover, but, once found, they prove to be more exact and elementary; they are at once infinitely numerous and infinitely small. It is only after these elementary resemblances are perceived that the higher, broader, more complex, and vaguer resemblances can be explained and assigned their proper value. Such an advance occurs whenever a number of fundamental differences that have previously been considered *sui generis* are resolved into combinations of

resemblances.   By this we do not mean
to say that science, as it advances, tends
to eliminate the fundamental differences,
or to diminish in number the unrepeated
aspects of phenomena.   For, while the
grosser and more obvious distinctions of
the mass dissolve under the searching
glance of the scientific observer, their
place is taken by others which are at
once more subtle and more profound, and
which multiply indefinitely, thus keeping
pace with the uniformities among the elements.

To apply this principle to the realm of
stars.   The science of astronomy dates
its origin from the moment when idle
or curious herdsmen noticed the peri-
odicity of the apparent revolutions of
the heavens, the rising and setting of
the stars, the circular courses of the
sun and moon, and the regular succession and recurrence of their positions in
the sky.   But in those early times certain stars appeared to be exceptions to

the general order of this one magnificent
revolution, namely, the *wandering* stars,
or planets; each of these was supposed
to follow a capricious course, which varied at every moment from its own previous course and that of the rest; later
on it was observed that there was some
regularity even in these anomalies.   Moreover, all stars — fixed and wandering, suns
and planets, including even the shooting
stars — were held to be essentially alike;
the only striking difference admitted was
between the sun and moon, on the one
hand, and all the others, on the other;
the two former being considered the only
really distinctive bodies in the firmament.

Now astronomy made its first step in
advance when for this one immense, apparent rotation of the entire heavens there
was substituted the conception of a host
of lesser real rotations, which differed
greatly from one another, and were in
no wise synchronous, but each of which
repeated itself indefinitely.   The second

step occurred when the peculiar distinctiveness of the sun vanished, to be replaced by a more subtle differentiation of each separate star, as the luminary of an invisible system, and centre of a planetary world analogous to the whirling concourse of our own planets. A still greater step in advance was made when the differences of apparent sidereal rotation which, though general and without exception, admitted irregularities in velocity, radius, eccentricity of orbit, etc., vanished before the Newtonian law of attraction — the latter representing all these periodicities of movement, from the most minute up to the greatest, and from the swiftest to the most slow, as due to endless and continual repetitions of one and the same fact, namely, attraction directly proportional to the mass and inversely to the square of the distance. And it were far better could we explain this fact in turn by the bold hypothesis, constantly rejected, yet ever besetting us anew, which attributes gravitation to the impacts of ether atoms, resulting from atomic vibrations of inconceivable minuteness and multiplicity.

Am I not correct, then, in saying that the science of astronomy has ever been concerned with resemblances and repetitions; that it started out with a single resemblance and repetition, immense and obvious in character, or with a small number at most, to arrive ultimately at an infinite number of infinitesimal resemblances and repetitions, real and elementary in character, which, when they appeared, furnished an explanation of the former?

Now does this necessarily imply, by the way, that the sky has lost any of its picturesqueness with the advances of astronomy? By no means. For, in the first place, the increased precision of apparatus and exactness of observations have enabled us to discern among the repetitions of stellar movements many differences, hitherto unperceived, which

have led to many new discoveries —
notably that of Leverrier. And in the
second place, our celestial horizon has
been constantly extended, and as its
vastness has increased, the differences
existing among various stars and groups
of stars in respect to size, velocity, and
physical characteristics have become much
more marked. The varieties of form
among the nebulæ have multiplied, and
when, at length, the spectroscope enabled
us to analyze in so extraordinary a manner the chemical composition of the
heavenly bodies, such differences were
found among them that men were led to
believe in the existence of radical differences between their respective inhabitants.
Finally, the geography of the nearest
planets has been revealed more clearly,
and, judging the rest from these (after
studying the canals of Mars, for instance),
we may conclude that each of the countless planets which circle above and
beneath us possesses its own special

C

characteristics, its own world-chart, and its own local features, and that these individual peculiarities give, there as here, a distinctive charm to each particular region, and no doubt engrave the love of country on the hearts of its inhabitants, whoever they may be.

Nor is this, in my opinion, all, though I shall only whisper it, lest I incur the serious charge of becoming a metaphysician. I believe that none of the above-mentioned differences, including even the mere variety of arrangement and random distribution of matter throughout space, can be explained on the theory of exactly similar atomic elements — an hypothesis so dear to chemists, who are in this respect the real metaphysicians; I do not see that Spencer's so-called law of the *instability of the homogeneous* explains anything. And hence, I believe that the only means of explaining this exuberant growth of individual differences upon the surface

of phenomena is by assuming that
they spring from a motley array of elements, each possessing its own individual
characteristics. Thus in the same way
that the mass *resemblances* have been
resolved into resemblances of detail, so
the gross and obvious mass *differences*
have been transformed into infinitely
minute differences of detail. And, just
as resemblances among the details alone
furnish an adequate explanation of
whatever resemblances appear in the
whole, so the elementary and invisible
distinctions, which I believe exist, alone
furnish an adequate explanation of those
greater and more apparent differences
that lend picturesqueness to the visible
universe.

So much for the physical world. In
the world of life the same is true. Imagine ourselves placed, like primitive
man, in the midst of a forest. All the
fauna and flora of a certain zone are
there, and we now know that the phe-

nomena revealed by these divers plants
and animals, however dissimilar they
may seem, resolve themselves ultimately
into a multitude of infinitesimal facts
which are summed up in the laws of
biology — whether it be animal or vegetable biology matters little, since the two
are at present classed together. But at
the outset men drew broad distinctions
between many things that we now place
in the same category, while they associated together many that we now
differentiate. The resemblances and repetitions which were then perceived, and
on which the infant science of the
organism was nourished, were superficial
and deceptive. Men classed together
plants that had no kinship, because their
leaves and general form revealed some
rough similarity; while they drew sharp
distinctions between plants of the same
family which were of different shape
and outline. The science of botany
made an advance when it learned the

relative value of different characteristics, and discovered that the most important of these (that is, the most repeated and significant, because accompanied by a host of other resemblances) are not those which are most obvious, but rather those which are most subtle and minute, especially those pertaining to the generative organs, such as the fact of having one cotyledon, two, or none at all.

And *biology*, the synthesis of zoölogy and botany, was born when the cell theory demonstrated that in both animals and plants the constantly repeated element is the cell — in the first place, the germ cell and then the others that proceed from it — when it showed that the fundamental phenomenon of life is an indefinite repetition by each cell of the functions of nutrition and activity, growth and fertilization, whose mould or cast each cell inherits and transmits in turn to its own posterity. This conformity to precedent may be called either habit or heredity. For simplicity's sake, let us call it all heredity, since habit is merely a sort of internal heredity, just as heredity is only externalized habit. Heredity, then, is the form of repetition appropriate to life, just as undulation, or periodic movement, is its physical, and imitation (as we shall find) its social form.

Thus we see that the progress of the science of living things has resulted in gradually removing all barriers raised on the side of their resemblances and repetitions, and substituting for these few, gross, and obvious resemblances, countless others, far more exact, though infinitely minute, which alone serve to explain the former. But at the same time hosts of new distinctions appear, and not only does the distinctive individuality of each organism become more salient, but we are forced also to admit certain differentiations of the cells themselves, and primarily of the germ cells; for while nothing is more similar in appearance than two germs, there is in reality scarcely any thing more different than their contents. After experiencing the insufficiency of the explanations proposed by Darwin and Lamarck to account for the origin of species, — whose kinship, descent, and evolution, however, is beyond dispute, — we must admit that the real cause of species lies hidden within the cells, the invention, as it were, of some primitive germ possessing an exceptionally fruitful individuality.

Well, then if we proceed to examine a city, a crowd, or an army, in place of the sky or forest, I maintain that the above reflections can be applied to the growth of social science as well as to astronomy and biology. Here, too, men have passed from hasty generalizations, founded on splendid analogies that were at once artificial and illusory, to generalizations supported by a mass of minute facts, whose resemblance to one another was comparatively clear and exact. So-

ciology has long been in process of construction. The first incoherent attempts
were made when, amid the distracting
chaos of social data, men discerned, or
believed that they discerned, something
periodic and regular. An early groping
after sociology appeared in the ancient
conception of a great cyclic year, at the
completion of which everything, in both
the social and natural worlds, should recur
in the same order. In place of this erroneously conceived single repetition of
the whole, which was welcomed by the
fanciful genius of Plato, Aristotle developed in his *Politics* certain repetitions of
detail (which, though often true, were
vague and difficult to grasp) concerning
what is most superficial, or certainly most
unimportant, in the social life, namely,
the order of succession of the several
forms of government. Arrested at this
point, the evolution of sociology began
again *ab ovo* in modern times. The *ri-
corsi* of Vico are the cycles of antiquity,

taken up and traced out anew, with somewhat less of the fantastic element. This
hypothesis and that of Montesquieu, on
the supposed similarity of civilizations developed in the same climate, are good
examples of the superficial and illusory
repetitions and resemblances on which
the science of sociology had to feed before it was fitted to receive more substantial nourishment. Chateaubriand, in his
Essai sur les révolutions, drew a lengthy
parallel between the English revolution
and the French revolution, and took
pleasure in dwelling on even the most
superficial resemblances. Others founded
elaborate theories on absurd analogies
drawn between the Punic and English
character, or between the Roman and
British empires. This attempt to confine
social facts within lines of development
which would compel them to repeat themselves *en masse* with merely insignificant
variations, has hitherto been the chief
pitfall of sociology, and that, whether

under the more rigid form conceived by Hegel, consisting of successions of triads, or under the more exact and scientific form that it has since received at the hands of the modern evolutionists. The latter, in discussing the transformations of laws (particularly the laws of family and of property) and the transformations of language, religion, industry, and art, have ventured to formulate general laws that would confine the progress of society, under these different aspects, to a constant passing and repassing along successive portions of the same arbitrary path. It remained to be discovered later that these supposed rules are honeycombed with exceptions, and that evolution, whether linguistic, legal, religious, political, economic, artistic, or moral, is not a single road, but a network of routes with many intersecting cross-ways.

Fortunately, screened and sheltered from view by these ambitious generalizations, certain less venturesome workers strove,

with greater success, to formulate other
more substantial laws concerning the details.   Among these should be mentioned
the linguists, the mythologists, and above
all the economists.   These specialists
in sociological fields discovered various
interesting relations among successive and
simultaneous facts, which recurred constantly within the limits of the narrow
domain they were examining.   In Adam
Smith's *Wealth of Nations*, Bopp's *Comparative Grammar of the Indo-European
Languages*, and Dietz's work, to cite but
three instances, we find a mass of observations of this sort, in which are pointed
out the resemblances running through
countless human actions — resemblances
in the pronunciation of certain conso-
nants and vowels, in buying and selling,
in the production and consumption of
certain articles, etc.   It is true that these
resemblances, when linguists endeavored
to formulate them further, gave rise to
very imperfect laws, conforming to a ma-

jority of cases only. But this is because the authors were in too great haste to formulate them, and did not wait to remove from its husk of partial truths the real kernel of absolute truth; to wit, the fundamental social fact which sociology is blindly pursuing, and which it must attain before it can really develop into a science.

In some quarters the feeling has existed that we must look to psychology for any general explanation of the laws and pseudo-laws of economics, language, mythology, etc. No man held to this view with greater force and clearness than John Stuart Mill. At the end of his *Logic* he represents sociology as a species of applied psychology. Unfortunately he did not analyze the concept carefully enough; and the psychology to which he looked for the key to social phenomena was merely individual psychology — the branch which studies the interrelations of impressions and imagery

in a single mind, believing that everything within this domain can be explained according to the *laws of association* of these elements. Thus conceived,
sociology became a sort of enlarged and
externalized English associationism, and
was in a fair way to lose its originality.
But it is not alone, nor chiefly to this
intra-cerebral psychology that we must
look for the fundamental fact of sociology, whose groupings and manifold
combinations make up our so-called simple phenomena, and form the data of
the particular social sciences; it is rather
in an *inter*-cerebral psychology, which
studies the rise of conscious relations
between two or more individuals, that
we must seek it. The relation of one
mind with another is, in fact, a distinctive event in the life of each; it is absolutely different from all their relations
with the rest of the universe, giving rise
to certain most unexpected states of
mind, that cannot be explained at all ac-

cording to the laws of physiological psychology. [1]

This relation between a subject and an object which is itself a subject — and not a perception in no way resembling the thing perceived — will not allow the idealistic sceptic to call in question the reality of the latter ; on the contrary, it means that we experience the sensation of a sentient thing, the volition of a conating thing, and the belief in a be-

[1] The experiments that have been made on hypnotic suggestion, and suggestion in the waking state, already furnish abundant material for the construction of an *inter*-cerebral psychology. I may be allowed to refer the reader to the applications of this still embryonic psychology which I have proposed throughout my works; more especially to the chapter in my *Laws of Imitation* (1890), entitled : *What is a society ?* which appeared previously, in November, 1884, in the *Revue philosophique ;* also to some pages of my *Philosophie pénale* (Philosophy of Punishment, 1890), on the formation of criminal crowds (in the chapter on *Crime*, p. 324 f. 1st French edition) ; my report entitled *Les crimes des foules* (The Crimes of Crowds), submitted at the Congress for Criminal Anthropology at Brussels, in August, 1892, and an article published in the *Revue des*

lieving thing, — the perception, in short, of a personality in which the perceiving personality is reflected, and which the latter cannot deny without denying itself.) This consciousness of a consciousness is the *inconcussum quid* which Descartes sought, and which the individual Self could not give him. Moreover, this unique relation is not a physical impulse given or received, nor is it the transmission of motor energy from the subject to

Deux Mondes for December, 1893, under the title of *Foules et sectes* (Crowds and Sects). The two latter studies were reprinted without change in my *Essais et mélanges sociologiques* (Sociological Essays and Miscellanies), which appeared in 1895 (Storck and Masson, publishers, Paris and Lyons). — I may observe, by the way, that the passage from the *Philosophie pénale*, cited above, which is merely a corollary of the chapter cited also from the *Laws of Imitation*, contains in substance, and very explicitly, the explanation of the phenomena of crowds which was developed afterward in the two other works mentioned ; this passage was published prior to the many interesting works that have recently appeared in France and abroad on the psychology of crowds. While this does not detract from their merit, it serves to answer a certain number of insinuations against me, which I have, moreover, fully met elsewhere.

an inanimate object or *vice versa*, according as we are dealing with an active or
passive state ; it is rather the transmission of something internal and mental,
which passes from one to other of
the two subjects, and that, curiously
enough, without being lost or in the
slightest degree diminished in the first.
But what manner of thing is it, that can
thus be transmitted from one mind to
another when they enter into psychological relation ? Is it their sensations or af-
fective states ? Evidently not; for these
are essentially incommunicable. The only
material that two subjects can communi-
cate to each other and consciously share,
with the result that they feel themselves
more closely united and more similar
thereby, are their notions and volitions,
their conclusions and aims. These are
forms which may still remain the same,
in spite of changes in content ; they are
products of that mental elaboration which
reacts almost equally well to any sensory

data.　Neither does such a form alter
perceptibly when it passes from a mind
of the visual type to one of the auditory
or motor type.　Thus the geometrical
ideas of one blind from birth are precisely the same as those of geometricians
endowed with the sense of sight.　And
similarly, a plan of campaign proposed
by one general whose temperament is
choleric and melancholy to others of mer-
curial and sanguine or passive and phleg-
matic dispositions may still remain the
same, if only the plan be concerned with
the same series of operations, and be desired by all with equal force, in spite of
the special and distinctive kinds of feeling that move each one separately to
desire it.　The strength of subjective
tendency, or mental eagerness, which I
call desire, like the strength of intellectual grasp, or mental adhesion and constraint, which I call belief, forms one
homogeneous and continuous stream.
Though variously tinged with the differ-

D

ent shades of affectivity pertaining to each separate mind, it nevertheless flows identically in each, now spreading and dividing, now uniting and contracting, and passing freely from one person to another, and from one perception to another in each person, without change.

To say that every real science possesses its own peculiar domain of elementary, countless, and infinitely small repetitions, is equivalent to saying that every real science is based on its own special qualities. Quantity, indeed, implies the possibility of one or more infinite series of infinitely small resemblances and repetitions. For this reason I have thought it well to insist, elsewhere, on the quantitative character of the two mental energies which, like two diverging rivers, water the two opposite slopes of the Self — its intellectual and its voluntary activity. If we deny their quantitative character, we declare sociology to be impossible. But we cannot deny it without ignoring the evidence; and a proof that the quantities in question are really social factors is seen in the fact that their quantitative character becomes more evident, and is grasped by the mind with greater clearness, the larger the quantities in which we see them, as when they manifest themselves in the shape of currents of popular belief or passion, or in traditional convictions and obstinacies of custom, embracing large groups of men. The more a group increases in size, the more the rise or fall of opinion, whether affirmative or negative, with respect to a given object, becomes capable of measurement. Such fluctuations of national belief or volition, indicated, for example, by the rise or fall of shares on the exchanges, then become comparable to the changes of temperature or atmospheric pressure, or to the varying force of a water-fall. It is for this reason that a science of statistics is more easily developed as states

grow larger. The particular aim of statistics being to discover and separate
real quantities from the confused general
mass of social facts, the success of the
science is greater the more it strives to
reach beyond the particular human acts
which it collects, and to measure the
total mass of beliefs and desires. The
statistics of stock-exchange values ex-
press the variations of public confidence
regarding the success of certain enterprises, such as the solvency of a certain
borrowing state, and the changes in
public desires and interests, to which
these loans or enterprises appeal. Industrial and agricultural statistics indicate the importance of the general needs
which demand the production of certain
articles, or the probable suitability of the
means set in operation to meet the demand. Judicial statistics, with their dry
enumerations of trials or offences, are of
interest to consult only because, between
their lines, we read the yearly increase

or decrease in the amount of public
desires engaged in proscribed or criminal
channels, such as the tendency to divorce
or theft; here, too, we see the degree in
which public hopes are affected by certain
kinds of trial or crime. The statistics of
population constitute, in most respects,
merely a biological study, having to do
with the numerical growth of the race
quite as much as with the duration and
progress of social institutions. But they
have a sociological import, in that they
indicate the increase or decrease of the
desire for paternity, maternity, and matri-
mony, as well as of the prevailing belief
that happiness is to be found in marriage
and the formation of fertile unions.

Under what conditions, then, is it legitimate to add together these forces of
belief and desire that lie stored up in
different individuals? Evidently, on condition that they possess the same object;
— that they have regard to the same idea
to be asserted, or the same action to be

executed. And what brought about this convergence, which renders the individual energies capable of combining to form a social unit? Can it have occurred spontaneously, by a chance encounter, or by some sort of preëstablished harmony? Decidedly not, except in a few instances; and even these apparent exceptions, were there time to follow them out, would be found to confirm the rule. This minute inter-agreement of minds and wills, which forms the basis of the social life, even in troublous times, — this presence of so many common ideas, ends, and means, in the minds and wills of all members of the same society at any given moment, — is not due, I maintain, to organic heredity, which insures the birth of men quite similar to one another, nor to mere identity of geographical environment, which offers very similar resources to talents that are nearly equal; it is rather the effect of that suggestion-imitation process which, starting from one primitive creature possessed of a single idea or act, passed this copy on to one of its neighbors, then to another, and so on. Organic needs and spiritual tendencies exist in us only as potentialities which are realizable under the most diverse forms, in spite of their primitive similarity; and, among all these possible realizations, the indications furnished by some first initiator who is imitated determine which one is actually chosen.

Let us return, then, to the fundamental social couple, to which I alluded just now; not the couple consisting of a man and woman in love, for this couple, in so far as it is sexual, is a purely vital phenomenon; but rather a couple composed of two persons, of either sex, one of whom exerts a mental influence upon the other. I maintain that the relation between these two persons is the one essential element in the social life, and that it always consists, at bottom, in an imitation of one by the other. But this

fact must be correctly interpreted, lest
it fall before the onslaught of foolish
and superficial objections. No one will
deny that whatever we say, do, or think,
once we are launched in the social life,
we are forever imitating some one else,
unless, indeed, we are ourselves making
an innovation — an event that rarely happens; it is easy, moreover, to show that
our innovations are, for the most part,
combinations of previous examples, and
that they remain outside of the social
life so long as they are not imitated.
There is not a word that you say, which
is not the reproduction, now unconscious,
but formerly conscious and voluntary, of
verbal articulations reaching back to the
most distant past, with some special ac-
cent due to your immediate surroundings.
There is not a religious rite that you
fulfil, such as praying, kissing the icon,
or making the sign of the cross, which
does not reproduce certain traditional ges-
tures and expressions, established through

imitation of your ancestors. There is
not a military or civil requirement that
you obey, nor an act that you perform in
your business, which has not been taught
you, and which you have not copied from
some living model. There is not a stroke
of the brush that you make, if you are a
painter, nor a verse that you write, if you
are a poet, which does not conform to the
customs or the prosody of your school, and
even your very originality itself is made up
of accumulated common-places, and aspires
to become common-place in its turn.

Thus, the unvarying characteristic of
every social fact whatsoever is that it
is imitative. And this characteristic belongs exclusively to social facts. On this
point, however, a specious objection has
been urged against me by Professor Giddings, who, nevertheless, with remarkable
ability, frequently adopts my own sociological standpoint. One society, he de-
clares, copies another; even enemies will
imitate one another; we borrow each

other's armaments, ruses of war and secrets of trade.   Hence, the domain of
imitativeness goes beyond that of *social-
ity*, and cannot be a special characteristic
of the latter.[1] But I am astonished at
such an objection on the part of an au-

[1] Giving to the word *imitation* the very wide meaning accorded to it in a recent and already celebrated
book on *Mental Development in the Child and the
Race*, by Mr. Baldwin, professor of psychology at Princeton University (U.S.A.) one might regard imitation as
the fundamental fact, not only of social and psychological life, but of organic life as well, where it would
appear as the necessary condition of habit and heredity.
As a matter of fact, however, the position of this keen
psychologist, far from contradicting my own view, is a
most striking illustration and confirmation of it.   Imitation between man and man, as I understand it, is
the consequence of imitation between one state and
another in the same man ; the latter is a species of
internal imitation which I had myself previously named
habit, and is evidently distinguished from the former
by characteristics clear enough to allow of their differentiation.   Professor Baldwin, who is first of all a biological psychologist, explains very correctly the organic
and mental genesis of imitation, and his task comes
to an end where that of the psychological sociologist
begins.   It is a pity that his book did not precede my
own on the *Laws of Imitation,* which would have

thor who regards the struggle between societies as a potent agency looking toward their ultimate socialization and merger into a broader society built up by their very battles. For is it not obvious that, to the extent that rival or hostile peoples assimilate their institutions, they themselves tend to coalesce? And hence, while it is perfectly true that each new act of imitation between individuals already associated tends to preserve and

gained by using his analyses. Nevertheless, the latter do not oblige me to amend in any way the laws and arguments formulated in my work. But in any case his book is the best answer I can make to those who accuse me of extending too widely the meaning of the word *imitation*. Professor Baldwin proves the contrary by extending it much further still. I learn, as these proofs are being corrected, that Professor Baldwin has recently applied his conceptions to sociology, and that by an independent route he has been led spontaneously to a position very analogous to that developed in my *Laws of Imitation*. [The work by Professor Baldwin referred to is his *Social and Ethical Interpretations in Mental Development* (Macmillans). In the second English edition of that work the author speaks of the relation of his researches to those of M. Tarde.— TR.]

strengthen the social bond, it is no less certain that such an act between individuals not yet associated prepares them for an association that may take place in the future, weaving by invisible threads something that will in time become a palpable bond. As regards some other objections that have been raised against me, I need not stop to consider them, since they arise from a very imperfect understanding of my ideas. They will disappear of their own accord if one will but place himself squarely at my standpoint. I refer the reader to my works for the elucidation of this matter.

But it is not enough merely to recognize the imitative character of every social phenomenon. I go further, and maintain that this imitative relation was not, in the beginning, as it often is later, a connection binding one individual to a confused mass of men, but merely a relation between two individuals, one of whom, the child, is in process of being introduced into the social life, while the other, an adult, long since socialized, serves as the child's personal model. As we advance in life, it is true, we are often governed by collective and impersonal models, which are usually not consciously chosen. But before we speak, think, or act as "they" speak, think, or act in our world, we begin by speaking, thinking, and acting as "he" or "she" does. And this *he* or *she* is always one of our own near acquaintances. Beneath the indefinite *they*, however carefully we search, we never find anything but a certain number of *he's* and *she's* which, as they have increased in number, have become mingled together and confused. Simple though this distinction be, it is nevertheless overlooked by those who deny that individual initiative plays the leading rôle in any social institution or undertaking. These writers imagine they are stating a weighty truth when they assert, for instance, that languages and religions are *collective* productions; that crowds, without a leader, constructed Greek, Sanscrit, and Hebrew, as well as Buddhism and Christianity, and that the formations and transformations of societies are always to be explained by the coercive action of the group upon its individual members (so that the latter, great and small alike, are always moulded and made subordinate to the former), rather than by the suggestive and contagious influence of certain select individuals upon the group as a whole. In reality, such explanations are quite illusory, and their authors fail to perceive that, in thus postulating a collective force, which implies the conformity of millions of men acting together under certain relations, they overlook the greatest difficulty, namely, the problem of explaining how such a general assimilation could ever have taken place. But this question is solved, if we extend the analysis, as I have done, to the intercerebral relation of two minds, the one reflecting the other. Only thus can we explain the partial agreements, the beating of hearts in unison, and the communions of soul, which, once brought about, and afterward perpetuated by tradition and the imitation of our ancestors, exert on the individual a pressure that is often tyrannical, but oftener still most salutary.[1] It is this relation, then, that the sociologist must adopt as his own peculiar data, just as the astronomer adopts the relation between two masses, the attracting and the attracted; it is here that he must seek the key to the social mystery; it is from this that he must endeavor to derive the few simple but universal laws, which may be distinguished amid the seeming chaos of history and human life.

[1] And do not forget this simple fact, that we enter upon the social life at a very early age. Hence, the child, who turns to others as a flower turns to the sun, feels the attraction of his family environment much more than its constraint. And in the same way, throughout his entire life, he continues to drink in these examples with avidity.

What I wish to call attention to at present is that sociology, thus understood, differs from the older conceptions that passed under the same name in the same way that our modern astronomy differs from that of the Greeks, or that biology, since the introduction of the cell theory, differs from the older natural history.[1] In other words, it rests on a foundation composed of real and elementary resemblances and repetitions which are infinitely numerous and extremely exact; these have replaced a

[1] This conception is, in fact, almost the exact opposite of the *unilinear evolutionists'* notion and of M. Durkheim's. Instead of explaining everything by the supposed supremacy of a *law of evolution*, which compels collective phenomena to reproduce and repeat themselves indefinitely in a certain order, — instead of thus explaining lesser facts by greater, and the part by the whole, — I explain collective resemblances of the whole by the massing together of minute elementary acts — the greater by the lesser and the whole by the part. This way of regarding phenomena is destined to work a transformation in sociology similar to that brought about in mathematics by the introduction of the infinitesimal calculus.

very small number of erroneous, or at least vague and deceptive analogies as primary material for scientific elaboration. And I may add, also, that, while social similarity has gained in extent and depth by this substitution, social differentiation has gained no less by the change. We must, from now on, no doubt, abandon such artificial differences as the "philosophy of history" established between successive peoples, each of which, like the chief actors of an immense drama, had his own predetermined rôle to play. Hence, it is no longer allowable to interpret those much-abused expressions: "the genius of a people or race," "the genius of a language," or "the genius of a religion," in the way that some of our predecessors, including even Renan and Taine, understood them. These embodiments of collective character, appearing under the guise of metaphysical entities or *idols*, were endowed with a fictitious personal

E

identity, which was, however, rather indefinite. Certain predispositions, supposed
to be invincible, for some particular gram-
matical types, religious conceptions, or
governmental forms, were freely attributed to them. On the other hand, they
were supposed to have an insuperable
repugnance to borrowing conceptions or
institutions from certain of their rivals.
The Semitic genius, for instance, was
held to be absolutely irreconcilable with
polytheism, parliamentary government, and
the analytic scheme of modern languages;
the Greek genius with monotheism; the
Chinese and Japanese genius with all
our European institutions and conceptions generally. If the facts protested
against such an ontological theory, they
were tortured to compel them to acknowledge its truth. It was useless to
call the attention of these theorists to
the radical transformations which a proselyting religion, a language, or an institution such as the jury system, undergoes,

when it spreads far beyond the bounda-
ries of its original race or people, in spite
of invincible obstacles that the "genius"
of other nations or races may seem
to rear against it. They replied by re-
vising the notion and distinguishing, at
least, between noble and inventive races,
which were alone endowed with the privilege of discovering and spreading discoveries, and races born to be in subjection,
which had no understanding of language,
religion, or ideas, and borrowed this material, or appeared to borrow it, from the
former. Moreover, they denied that such
a proselyting conquest of one civilization
or race genius over another could pass
certain bounds, as, for example, in the
Europeanization of China and Japan.
As regards the last, the contrary has
since proved itself true, and it will soon
prove true of the Middle Kingdom also.

Sooner or later, one must open his eyes
to the evidence, and recognize that the
genius of a people or race, instead of

being a factor superior to and dominating
the characters of the individuals (who have
been considered its offshoots and ephemeral manifestations) is simply a convenient
label, or impersonal synthesis, of these
individual characteristics; the latter alone
are real, effective, and ever in activity;
they are in a state of continual fermen-
tation in the bosom of every society,
thanks to the examples borrowed and exchanged with neighboring societies to
their great mutual profit. The impersonal, collective character is thus the
product rather than the producer of the
infinitely numerous individual characters;
it is their composite photograph, and
must not be taken for their mask. We
shall certainly lose nothing of that social
picturesqueness which makes the histo-
rian an artist, when, having cleared up,
rather than cleared away, this phantas-
magoria of great historic actors called
Egypt, Rome, Athens, etc., we perceive
behind it a swarm of individual innova-

tors, each *sui generis*, stamped with his own distinctive mark, and recognizable among a thousand. Hence I conclude, once more, that in adopting this socio-logical standpoint we shall have done precisely what all the other sciences have done as they progressed, namely, replaced the small number of erroneous or un-certain resemblances and differences by countless real and exact ones; this is a great gain for both the artist and the scientist; but it is a still greater gain for the philosopher, who, if he is to retain a distinctive function, must undertake a synthesis of the two.

A few remarks more. So long as none of the elementary astronomical facts, such as the Newtonian Law, or at least that of elliptical orbits, had been discovered, there were many heterogeneous bits of astronomical knowledge,— a science of the moon, *selenology*, and a science of the sun, *heliology*, — but there was no astronomy. So long as there had been no discovery of the elementary facts of chemistry (affinity and combination in definite proportions), there were many bits of chemical knowledge, and the special chemistries of iron, tin, copper, etc., but no science of chemistry. So long as men had not discovered the essential fact of physics, the undulatory transmission of molecular movement, there were many bits of physical knowledge,—optics, acoustics, thermology, electrology, — but no physics. Physics became physico-chemistry, the science of all inorganic nature, when the possibility was seen of explaining all things by the fundamental laws of mechanics ; that is, when men believed that they had discovered the elementary inorganic facts, in the equality and contrariety of action and reaction, the conservation of energy, the reduction of all forces to forms of motion, the mechanical equivalent of heat, electricity, light, etc. Finally, before the discovery of the analogies existing between animals and plants from the standpoint of reproduction, there was not a single botany and a single zoölogy, but different botanies and zoölogies, which might have been named hippology, cynology, etc. The discovery of the above-mentioned resemblances gave only partial unity to these various scattered sciences — these *disjecta membra* of the coming biology. Biology was really born when the cell theory appeared, exhibiting the elementary fact of life, namely, that the functions of the cell (or histological element) and its proliferation are continued by the germ, itself a cell, so that nutrition and generation were thus seen from the same angle of vision.

And now we are about to construct, in like manner, a social science, to succeed the social sciences. For there were social sciences, at least in outline, — the beginnings of political science, linguistics, comparative mythology, æsthetics, and ethics, together with a political economy already well advanced, — long before even an embryo of sociology existed. Sociology requires a fundamental social fact. She requires it so urgently that, so long as she had not succeeded in discovering any (possibly because the fact was tearing out her eyes, if I may be pardoned the expression), she was dreaming of such a fact, and imagining it in the form of one of those idle, imaginary resemblances that beset the cradle of every science ; she believed herself to be asserting a highly instructive fact when she pictured society as a great organism, where the individual (or, according to others, the family) was the social cell, and every form of social activity represented some sort of cellular function. I have already made many efforts, in company with most other sociologists, to sweep away this obstructive notion from the path of the new science. Yet a word further on the subject may be in place.

Scientific knowledge feels so strongly the need of relying on resemblances and repetitions before all else, that, when none

are within its grasp, it actually creates imaginary ones to supply the place of the
real; among these we must class the fam-
ous simile of the social organism, together
with many other symbolic concepts that
have attained a like ephemeral usefulness.
At the starting-point of every science, as
at the starting-point of every literature, allegory plays an important rôle.   In mathematics, we find the allegorical vision of
Pythagoras and Plato preceding the solid
generalizations of Archimedes. Astrology
and magic — the one the gateway to astronomy, the other the early babblings of
chemistry — are founded on the postulate
of *universal allegory*, rather than that of universal analogy; they assume a pre-estab-
lished harmony between the positions of
certain planets and the destinies of certain
men, between some fictitious act and some
real one, between the nature of a chemical substance and that of the heavenly
body whose name it bears, and so on.
We must not forget the symbolic character

of primitive proceedings, for example, the *actio legis*, in the Roman code, that early groping after jurisprudence. We should note also (since theology, like jurisprudence, became a science some time ago, the excessive application of figurative meanings to biblical stories by the earlier theologians, who saw in the history of Jacob a copy by anticipation of the history of Christ, or regarded the love of the husband and wife in the *Song of Solomon* as symbolic of the love of Christ and his church. The mediæval science of theology began in this way, just as modern literature began with the *Romance of the Rose*. It is a long step from such notions to the *Summa* of St. Thomas Aquinus. Even down to the present century we find lingering traces of this symbolic mysticism; they appear in good Father Gratry's works, now long forgotten, yet worthy to be resurrected on account of their Fénelonian grace of style. Father Gratry believed that the solar system symbolized the successive relations of the soul and God, as the former, according to his notion, revolved around the latter. For him, again, the circle and the ellipse symbolized the whole of ethics, a science which he believed to be inscribed in hieroglyphics upon the conic sections.

I have no desire, of course, to compare these eccentric views with the partly substantial and always serious development which Herbert Spencer and, more recently, M. René Worms and M. Novicow, following Comte, have effected in the theory of the "social organism." I appreciate fully the merit and temporary usefulness of such work, even though I criticise it. But, to generalize now what precedes, I believe I have the right to lay down the following proposition: The advance of every science consists in suppressing *external* likenesses and repetitions, — that is, comparisons of the peculiar material of that science with other things, — and replacing them by *internal* likenesses and repetitions,

— that is, comparisons of that material with itself, as it appears in its many copies and under its different aspects. The notion of the social organism, which regards the nation as a plant or animal, corresponds to that of vital automatism, which regards the plant or animal as a piece of mechanism. It is not this hollow and far-fetched comparison of the living body with a piece of mechanism that has advanced biology, but rather a comparison of plants with one another, animals with one another, and living bodies with one another.[1] So, too, it is not by comparing societies with organisms that sociology has already made great steps in advance and is

[1] Similarly, it was not the Pythagorean comparisons between mathematics and various other sciences that advanced mathematics ; such comparisons were absolutely sterile, while the bringing together of two branches of mathematics, geometry and algebra, under the guidance of Descartes, was most fruitful. And it was only when the infinitesimal calculus was invented and men went back to the indecomposable mathematical element whose continuous repetition explains all, that the immense fertility of mathematics fully appeared.

destined to make still greater ones in the future, but by comparing various societies with one another; by noting the endless coincidences between distinct national evolutions, from the standpoint of language, jurisprudence, religion, industry, art, and custom; and above all by attending to those imitations between man and man which furnish an analytic explanation of the collective facts.

After these lengthy preliminaries, the time has come when it would be in place to set forth the general laws governing imitative repetition, which are to sociology what the laws of habit and heredity are to biology, the laws of gravitation to astronomy, and the laws of vibration to physics. But I have fully treated this subject in one of my works, *The Laws of Imitation*, to which I may refer those who are interested in the subject. Nevertheless, I think it important to bring out here what I did not make sufficiently clear, namely, that in the last analysis all these laws flow from a higher principle — the tendency of an example, once started in a social group, to spread through it in geometrical progression, provided the group remains homogeneous. By this term *tendency*, however, I do not mean anything mysterious; on the contrary, it denotes a very simple thing. When, for instance, in a group, the need is felt of expressing a new idea by a new word, the first individual who finds an expressive image fitted to meet that need has only to pronounce it, when immediately it is echoed from one neighbor to another, till soon it trembles on every lip in the group in question, and later spreads even to neighboring groups. Not that we mean by this, in the least, that the expression is endowed with a soul which causes it to send forth rays in this manner, any more than the physicist, in saying that a sound-wave tends to radiate in the air, means to endow this mere form with a personal, eager, and ambitious force.[1] It is only another way of saying, in the one case, that the motor forces inherent in the molecules of air have found, in this vibratory repetition, a channel into which they drain; and, in the other case, that a special need felt by the human beings of the group in question has found satisfaction in this imitative repetition, which enables them, as a concession to their indolence (the analogue of physical *inertia*), to escape the trouble of inventing for themselves. However, there is no doubt of the tendency to spread in geometrical proportion, though this tendency is often hindered by obstacles of various sorts, so that it is quite rare, though not extremely so, for statistical diagrams relating to the spread of a

[1] Or any more than the naturalist, when he says that a species tends to increase in geometrical proportion, regards the type-form as possessing an energy and aim independent of the sun, the chemical affinities, and the various forms of physical energy, instead of being simply their channel.

new industrial invention to show a regular progression. Now what are the obstacles referred to? There are some that arise from differences of climate and race, but these are not the most important. The greatest impediment to the spread of a social innovation and its consolidation into a traditional custom is some other equally expansive innovation which it encounters during its course, and which, to employ a physical metaphor, interferes with it. In fact, every time any one of us hesitates between two modes of verbal expression, two ideas, two beliefs, or two modes of action, it means that an interference between two imitation-rays takes place in him; these rays have started from different generating centres, often widely separated in space and time (namely, certain individual inventors and imitators of primitive times), and have spread onward, till they reached the individual in question. And how is his difficulty solved? What are the influences that decide his course? There are influences, as I have said elsewhere, of two kinds: logical and extralogical. I should add that even the latter are logical in one sense of the term; for while, between two examples, the plebeian selects blindly that of the patrician, the countryman that of the townsman, and the provincial that of the Parisian — a phenomenon which I have called the descent of imitation from the top to the bottom of the social ladder — this very imitation, however blind it be, is influenced in every case by the superiority attributed to the model, which makes the example of the latter appear in the eyes of the form to possess some social authority over him. The same is true when, as between his ancestors and some foreign innovator, primitive man does not hesitate to prefer the example of the former, whom he esteems infallible; and the same is true, only conversely,

F

when, in a similar perplexity, the deni-
zen of our modern cities, persuaded in
advance that the new is always preferable to the old, makes precisely the
opposite choice. Nevertheless, the case
where the opinion of the individual is
founded on reasons extrinsic to the nature of the models compared and the
two ideas or acts in opposition, should
be carefully distinguished from the case
where he chooses in virtue of a judgment resting on the intrinsic character
of these two ideas or volitions; hence,
the term *logical* should be reserved for
the influences that decide him in the
latter case.

I need not discuss this question further
at present, since in the next chapter I
shall have occasion to speak again of
these logical and teleological duels, which
constitute the fundamental terms of social
opposition. Let me only add here that
the interferences of imitation-rays are not
always impediments to each other's pro-

gress; often they result in mutual alli-
ances, which serve to accelerate and enlarge the radiation; sometimes they are
even responsible for the rise of some
generic idea, which is born of their encounter and combination within a single
head, as we shall see in the chapter de-
voted to social adaptation.

CHAPTER II

THE OPPOSITION OF PHENOMENA

HEORETICALLY, the repetition aspect of phenomena is the most important one to consider; but their opposition aspect is of greater practical interest, viewed from the standpoint of scientific applicability. Yet, from the days of Aristotle down to the present, this latter has been either completely misunderstood, or at least hidden from view amid the disordered mass of other differences.

Here, as in the former case, we may say that the progress of science consists in doing away with the small number of superficial gross oppositions that were perceived or imagined at first, and replacing them by countless profounder and subtler oppositions, that are exceedingly difficult to discover; and that it involves the substitution of internal for external oppositions in the subject under discussion. We may further add that it also serves to clear away certain apparent dissymmetries or asymmetries, and substitute for them numerous others, deeper hidden and more instructive.

Consider the oppositions existing in the realm of stars. Day and night and heaven and earth were the first antitheses proposed; on these the theological cosmogonies, those embryos of astronomy and geology, just beginning life, or striving to begin it, subsisted. The next oppositions to appear possessed more truth, but they were still misunderstood, or were entirely subjective or superficial: thus we find zenith and nadir (which is merely the old antithesis between *up* and *down* carried to its logical conclusion); the four cardinal points of the compass set over against one another in pairs ; winter and summer, spring and autumn, morning and evening, midday and midnight, the first and last quarters of the moon, and so on. All these oppositions were retained, it is true, even after the science grew older ; nevertheless they lost much of their original importance and significance. The west is not, for savage races, as it is for us, merely a relative direction, defined with respect to our position as we face the so-called polar star ; to them the west is the region of happiness after death, the everlasting abode of souls ; for others, the east fulfils this same rôle. Hence, their ritual determines the direction that temples and tombs shall face. The first and last quarters of the moon have assuredly not the important imaginary meaning attributed to them by the superstitious tillers of the soil in primitive times, or even by our own peasants. According to them, the new moon is the direct cause of rapid growth, while the old moon hinders the

growth of whatever is planted during one
or other of its two phases. This is a ves-
tige of the old antithesis between *dies
fasti* and *dies nefasti*.

Thus, these oppositions have been pre-
served, but with a superficial and conven-
tionalized meaning. Others, again, have
been eliminated, as, for example, the opposition between celestial and terrestrial,
and between sun and moon; while the
emphasis, as in the former instances, has
been transferred to other oppositions,
possessing a far deeper meaning. First,
the discovery of the elliptic, parabolic,
or hyperbolic character of the orbits described by stars, planets, and comets led to
the perception of the complete symmetry
of the two halves of the orbit on either
side of the major axis. (That is, *complete*,
aside from certain perturbations which are
reciprocal repetitions of the curves of one
star by another, within the same system.)
Next, it was observed that the ellipses of
the planets' courses increased and de-

creased alternately, with great regularity, oscillating about a certain position of equilibrium. Finally, the most profound, widespread, and enduring opposition in astronomy, and the basis of all the rest, is the equality of the attraction exerted *upon* every mass and molecule and that exerted *by* it. Each attracts and is attracted in like degree. This is one of the most beautiful illustrations of the physical law of universal opposition, called the law of the equality and contrariety of action and reaction.

Physics and chemistry, like astronomy, began with pseudo-oppositions. The four elements imagined by the early physicists were contrasted with one another in pairs: water as against fire, and air as against earth. Innate antipathies were supposed to exist between certain substances. More wholesome ideas respecting the true nature of physical and chemical opposition were reached when men discovered the characteristics of bases and

acids, and the sort of opposition between
them ; still more so, when they discovered
the two opposite kinds of electricity and
the polarity of light. The concept of
polarity, which has played so important
a rôle in physico-chemical theories,
marked a great advance over previous
conceptions, until it was itself explained
by the concept of undulations, into which
its effects have been resolved, or are in
a fair way to be resolved. And just as
light, heat, and electricity appear to be
spherical or linear propagations of vibrations at once infinitely small and infinitely
rapid, so there is a tendency to consider
chemical combination as an harmonious
union and interlacing of waves. But
here we touch on the domain of *adaptation.* Even attraction itself has often
been explained as due to the impacts of
ether vibrations. However this may be,
it is nevertheless certain that the elliptical orbits of the stars are comparable, except in respect to dimensions, to physical

vibrations, since the molecules follow an elongated elliptical course, and a rhythm of undulation exists in both cases. In short, we observe how the field of oppositions has been extended and broadened by the progress of science, and how, in place of *qualitative* oppositions, there have appeared those exact and rhythmic *quantitative* oppositions which form the texture of the world-fabric. The wonderful symmetry of crystalline forms in every chemical substance constitutes a graphic interpretation and visual expression of the rhythmic oppositions between those countless movements of which it is the embodiment. And must we not also look to this rhythm of the internal movements of a body for the ultimate explanation of Mendelejeff's law, which shows us that the groups of substances form a number of successive, rising scales, like a piano from whose keyboard some keys here and there are missing, which we shall replace from time to time?

But while the evolution of the physical sciences revealed certain oppositions and symmetries that were at once clearer, more profound, and more satisfactory in the explanations they afforded, it also brought to light certain asymmetries, lack of rhythm, or *inoppositions*, of far greater importance. It showed, for example, that in all our solar system there is no planetary body with a retrograde motion, that is, with a motion in the opposite direction to that of the general run of planets; the only exception to this is in the case of certain satellites. The form of the nebulæ revealed by our telescopes is often unsymmetrical. We have not the slightest reason for believing that any relation of symmetry exists between the evolution and dissolution of a solar system (if, indeed, there be a dissolution), or between the formation of the successive geological strata in a planet, and its final separation into fragments, if the ideas of M. Stanilas Meunier on this point be accepted. With all the progress that astronomy has made, the scattering and grouping of the stars in the heavens remains, as before, a mighty example of picturesque disorder and randomness. Indeed, this spectacle of sublime disorder appears more striking as greater advances have been made in the knowledge of forces in equilibrium and symmetrically opposed, which form their apparent constituents. What astronomer of to-day would dream, like the ancients, of an antiworld, or *antichthon*, where everything exhibited the reverse of the terrestrial order? Again, as the geography of our planet becomes better known, we are more than ever struck with the absence of symmetry in the form of its continents and mountain chains, and Élie de Beaumont's notion of the *réseau pentagonal* no longer attracts any one. The advance of crystallography has brought to notice dissymmetries hitherto unperceived, whose importance have been set in relief by the work of Pasteur. But I can merely mention this subject.

In the realm of life, the grosser and more obvious oppositions, such as life and death, youth and old age, were the first to be observed; these were the earliest correspondences noted between animals and plants, and formed the rudiments of general biology. Moreover, it was impossible not to notice the symmetry of living forms, so striking and strange because of its universality. Yet, here, too, fancy gave birth to a host of oppositions unreal or without value. Among them may be mentioned the angels and demons, both of which were conceived as being superior species of animals. Similarly, for the savage, and sometimes even for the uncultured man of our day, the most important opposition in the realm of life is between things that are good to eat and those that are not, that is, between nutritious and poisonous plants, and between useful and harmful animals. Here we have an opposition that is real in a subjective sense, but imaginary in so far as it is believed to hold objectively, as it is by ignorant men of all races. Physicians for a long time conceived of sickness and health as two exactly opposite states, and believed that the causes of sickness were the exact reverse of the causes of health. The error of homœopathy was due, at bottom, to this illusion. Sickness and health, as thus conceived, are merely verbal entities, which the advances of physiology have cast aside; pathological deviations are phases of the physiological functions, instead of being opposed to them. The dissolution of the individual was also regarded as the inverse of evolution, old age being considered as a return of childhood. This view was only finally eliminated when embryology brought to light the passage through a series of ancestral forms, which have, obviously, no inverse analogue in the successive stages of senile decay.

Long after the sciences dealing with life were organized, physiologists still imagined a certain artificial opposition, as well as a scientific one, which they held existed between the animal and vegetable kingdoms. In their eyes, vegetable respiration was exactly the reverse of animal respiration ; the former destroyed what the latter produced, namely, the union of oxygen and carbon. Comparative physiology, as developed by Claude Bernard and others, demonstrated the superficial character of this opposition, and established the fundamental unity of the two kingdoms, showing them to be not inverse, but divergent. On the other hand, the growth of knowledge eliminated these false or vague oppositions between different groups of beings, different beings, and different entities within the same being, and substituted countless real though infinitesimal oppositions in the inmost nature of the tissues; for example, the oxidation and deoxidation of each cell, or the gain and loss of energy. Here, again, opposition appears most fundamental and fruitful under the form of rhythm, rather than in the guise of strife.

But at the same time, certain new and more subtle dissymmetries were brought to light. To cite but a single instance, the study of the cerebral functions, when it demonstrated the localization of the speech function in the left hemisphere, established a very important dissymmetry of function between the two halves of the brain. And this is not the only case where symmetry of form between corresponding organs of the two sides of the body, such as the right and left hand, the right and left eye, etc., has been found to cover a wide dissymmetry or asymmetry in their function. Besides this, as I said above, that very ancient hypothesis, so plausible in appearance, that the dissolution of living beings and types must be exactly opposite to the manner of their evolution, was forced to surrender before the advances of observation. And this lack of symmetry between the two opposite slopes of life, — its ascent and descent, — whether in individuals or in the species, has an important meaning; for it goes to show that life is not a mere play — a see-saw of forces, so to speak — but rather an act of going forward, and that the notion of progress is not an idle one. It enables us to view the oppositions of phenomena, with all their symmetries, struggles, and rhythms, and in like manner their repetitions, as simply instruments or *mean terms* of progress.

Sociology gives rise to analogous reflections. In the beginning (for in some respects the science is quite ancient), it started as a mythology, and after the manner of mythologies it was satisfied with explaining everything in history by

G

fantastic struggles, or imaginary wars of
enormous dimensions between good and
evil deities, gods of light and darkness,
or heroes and monsters. But metaphysics made undue use of contests, quite as
much as mythology; for the metaphysicians also imagined oppositions between
direct and reverse series, and held that
developments of humanity in one direction were followed by developments in
the contrary direction. On this point
Plato and the Hindu philosophers join
hands. Hegel, with his sweeping generalizations, his marshalling of different
races under the banner of Antagonistic
Ideas, and Cousin, with his imaginary
antithesis between Oriental Infinity and
Greek Finity, are excellent examples of
the sociological antinomies of the past.
All this has vanished; and to-day, especially after the amazing Europeanization
of Japan within the past few years, we
do not even venture to set the supposed
immutability of the Asiatics over against

the supposed innate progressiveness of the European races.

The political economists have already rendered social science a noteworthy service, by substituting for war, as the keynote of history, the factor of *competition*, which is a species of war not only modified and mollified, but at the same time dwarfed and manifolded. Finally, if our point of view be adopted, the competition of desires and beliefs must be regarded as constituting the basis of what political economists call the competition between consumers and the competition between producers. Generalizing this struggle, and extending it to every form existing in the social life, — linguistic, religious, political, artistic, and moral, as well as industrial, — we see that the *really fundamental social opposition* must be sought for in the bosom of the social individual himself, whenever he *hesitates* between adopting or rejecting a new pattern offered him, whether in the way of phraseology, ritual, concept, canon of art, or conduct. This hesitation, this miniature internal battle, which is renewed a million times every moment of a nation's life, constitutes the infinitely minute and infinitely fruitful opposition that underlies history. It is producing a peaceful but far-reaching revolution in the realm of sociology.

At the same time, and from this same standpoint, the auxiliary and subordinate character of social opposition (even in its psychological form) is shown by the appearance of a large number of asymmetries and dissymmetries that did not at first reveal themselves. I find it necessary to distinguish (and on this point I find no one to contradict me) between the *reversible* and the *irreversible* in every species of social fact; and of these the irreversible have always proved the more important category; as, for example, the series of discoveries in science and the industrial life. Again, for the very reason that the life of each social individual is composed of such numerous psychological oppositions, there has been a real accentuation of his individual characteristics, or his personality, something which has no antithesis, and for which the so-called genius of a people, or, if you prefer, the genius of a language, or a religion, is merely a collective and abbreviated form of expression. We find, also, that the æsthetic side of the social life, the side on which it can neither be compared nor opposed to anything, is supported by this very interplay of infinite minute oppositions, which I have just described.

But this summary glance is very incomplete. It is important to examine more closely this subject, which has been so little explored, though deserving of the greatest attention. Let us, first of all, come to a clear understanding with regard to the different meanings of the word *opposition*. In my work on *Uni-*

versal Opposition I proposed a definition
and a classification to which I may be
permitted to refer. Let us sum the matter up briefly from our present point of
view. Opposition is erroneously conceived by the average thinker as the
maximum degree of difference. In reality, it is a very special kind of repetition, namely, of two similar things that
are mutually destructive by virtue of their
very similarity. In other words, opposites or contraries always constitute a
couple or duality; they are not opposed
to each other as beings or groups of
beings, for these are always dissimilar
and, in some respect, *sui generis;* nor
yet as *states* of a single being or of different beings, but rather as tendencies
or *forces.* For, if we regard certain
forms or certain states, such as concave
and convex, pleasure and pain, heat and
cold, as opposites, it is by reason of
the real or assumed contrariety of the
forces which produce these states.

Thus we see that it is necessary to eliminate from the start, as so many pseudo-oppositions, all the antitheses of mythology and the philosophy of history which are based on assumed *natural* contrarieties; for example, the contrarieties between two nations, two races, or two forms of government (such as republic and monarchy, to cite certain Hegelians in this matter); or between occident and orient, two religions (such as Christianity and Mohammedanism), or two families of languages (such as the Semitic and Indo-European). These contrasts chance to be partially true, if we take into consideration the manner in which the things in question deny or affirm the same notion, and desire or reject the same end, under certain more or less ephemeral circumstances. But if the antipathy of these things for each other be regarded as essential, absolute, and innate, as many ancient philosophers seemed to believe, they are wholly chimerical.

Thus, every real opposition implies a relation between two forces, tendencies, or *directions*. But the phenomena by means of which these two forces become actualities are of two kinds, — qualitative and quantitative, — that is, they may be composed of either heterogeneous or homogeneous parts. A series made up of heterogeneous factors is a species of evolution that can always be *conceived of* (whether rightly or wrongly) as reversible, or capable of going back by following the same road in precisely the opposite direction. For example, if a chemist, taking a piece of wood and going through a series of operations, ends by extracting brandy from it, this does not of course imply that it would be possible to reconstruct the piece of wood by a series of inverse operations; yet if this is not a possibility, it is at least conceivable. And this was the dream of the ancient philosophers with respect to the transformations of humanity. A series made up of homogeneous factors is an evolution of a special sort, known as increase or decrease, wax or wane, rise or fall. Without entering too minutely into the facts, we must notice how, as social science develops with the advance of civilization, instances of exact and measurable oppositions of this sort continue to appear and multiply, giving us fluctuations of the stock market and statistical diagrams on which are registered in wave-like curves the rise and fall of some particular security, of some particular species of crime, of suicide, the birth-rate, marriage, or thrift as measured by the returns of the savings banks, insurance companies, etc.

The distinction just made is between oppositions of series (evolution and counter-evolution) and oppositions of degree (increase and diminution). A still more important category to be considered consists of oppositions of *sign*, or, if we prefer, *diametrical* oppositions. Although these last are often confused with the preceding in the language of mathematics, in which plus and minus symbolize increase and diminution as well as positive and negative directions, it is nevertheless true that the alternate increase and decrease of a force acting always in the same direction constitutes a very different sort of opposition from that of two forces, one of which acts from A toward B, and the other from B toward A, both along the same straight line. Similarly, the contrast between the increase and decrease of a credit balance must not be confused with the contrast between such a credit and an equal debt; and the growth or diminution of the tendency to theft or crime, in a given society, is quite a different thing from the antithesis between this tendency and the tendency to charity and philanthropy. In order to give at once a psychological explanation of these and many other social contrasts, we may observe that an increase followed by a diminution of our *affirma-tive* belief in a notion, whether religious or scientific, legal or political, is quite a different matter from our affirmation followed by our *rejection* of this same idea, and that an increase followed by a diminution of our desire for something, for instance our love for a woman, is quite a different matter from a desire followed by a repugnance to the same object, such as our love toward this woman and then our hatred of her. It is certainly interesting to note that each of these subjective quantities, belief and desire, possesses two opposite signs, the positive and negative, and that in this respect they admit of comparison with objective quantities, such as mechanical forces which act in opposite directions along the same straight line. Space is so constituted as to admit of an infinity of couples whose members are opposed to each other in direction, and our consciousness is so constituted as to admit of an infinity of affirmations opposed to negations, or an infinity of desires opposed to repugnances, each having precisely the same object. Except for these two unique instances, whose coincidence is remarkable, the universe would know neither war nor discord, and all the tragic side of life would be both impossible and inconceivable.

One observation is necessary, however. The oppositions of every sort — of series, degrees, or signs — may take place between terms that find expression either in one and the same being (whether molecule, organism, or *self*), or in two different beings (molecules, masses, organisms, or human consciousnesses). But we must distinguish carefully between these two cases. This is of primary importance for the sake of another distinction that is no less essential, namely, the distinction between the case where the terms are simultaneous and the case where they are successive. In the former there is a collision, strife, and then equilibrium; in the latter there is alternation and rhythm. In the former there is always destruction and loss of energy; in the latter there is neither. Now when any oppositions whatsoever, whether of series, degrees, or signs, occur in two different beings, they may be either simultaneous or successive — either strife or rhythm. But when both of their terms belong to one and the same being, body, or self, they can only be both simultaneous and successive if they are oppositions of signs. As for the oppositions of series and degrees under this hypothesis, they admit only of a succession or alternation of terms. For instance, it is impossible for the velocity of a body moving in a given direction to increase and diminish at the same time; it can only do so successively. But it may well happen that it is impelled at the same time by two distinct forces to move in two opposite directions; this is the case of equilibrium, which is often characterized by a symmetry of opposite forms, notably in the case of crystals. Similarly, it is impossible for the love of a man for a woman to increase and diminish at the same time: such a thing can only occur alternately; but it may easily occur for him to love and hate the same woman at the same time — an antinomy of the heart that finds illustration in many crimes of passion. Again, it is impossible for the religious faith of a man to increase and diminish at the same time: this can only occur successively; but it may easily happen that he has in his thoughts, at the same time, though often without being himself aware of it, a vigorous affirmation and a no less vigorous if implicit denial of certain dogmas; that he holds at once a certain Christian belief, and a certain worldly or political prejudice which is opposed to it. Finally, it is evidently impossible for one and the same molecule to pass through a certain series of chemical transformations and the inverse series at the same time, or for the same man to be experiencing the same

psychological states in two opposite orders
at the same time; that can only occur successively. But, on the other hand, nothing
is more common than to observe, in a system of bodies, astronomical or otherwise,
one body passing from aphelion to perihelion, while another body is passing at the
same time from perihelion to aphelion; or
one body that is accelerating its speed,
while another is slackening it. And nothing
is more common than to observe, in a society, one person's ambition or faith increasing while the ambition or faith of another
is declining; or, again, one person who, in
making a round trip, passes through a
certain series of visual impressions, while
another, taking the opposite route, passes
through the same series of impressions in
the inverse order.

A discussion of each of the species of
oppositions here pointed out would carry
us beyond our limits. We must be satisfied with a few general reflections. First,
then, if *external oppositions* exist (for so we

may term the oppositions of tendencies between different beings or men), they are rendered possible by the fact that *internal oppositions* (between different tendencies within the same being or man) exist or may exist. This applies to oppositions of series and degrees as well as to oppositions of sign, but more particularly to the latter. If certain men or groups of men are developing in one direction, while other men or groups of men are developing in the contrary direction, it is because each individual man can either develop or counter-develop in this way; as, for example, in the transition from naturalism to idealism, or from idealism to naturalism, in art, and from an aristocracy to a democracy, or *vice versa*, in government, etc. If religious faith is on the increase among certain races or classes, while among others it is on the decline, it is because the consciousness of each individual man admits of either an increase or a diminution in the intensity of religious faith. Finally, if

there exist political parties and religious
sects which affirm and desire what other
parties and sects deny and reject, it is because the mind and heart of each individual man is capable of containing both the
yes and the *no*, the *pro* and the *con*, with
respect to any given concept or aim.

Nevertheless, I am far from wishing
to identify *external* with *internal* contests.
In one sense they are incompatible ; for
it is only when the internal struggle is
ended, when the individual, after having been pulled hither and thither by
contrary influences, has made his choice,
and adopted a certain opinion or resolu-
tion rather than some other — it is only
when he has made peace with himself —
that war between himself and those who
have made the opposite choice becomes
possible. Nor is this of itself sufficient
to bring about such a war. The individual must *know*, in addition, that the others
have chosen the opposite of what he has
himself chosen. Without this, any ex-

H

ternal opposition of contraries, whether
simultaneous or successive, would be
practically non-existent, for it would present none of those characteristics that
render an external struggle really effective. To bring about religious war or
strife, it is essential for every adherent
of one faith to know that the adherents
of some other faith deny exactly what he
affirms ; and this negation must be placed
side by side in his consciousness with his
own affirmation, not as though adopted
imitatively, but rather as being definitely
rejected by him, and hence redoubling
the intensity of his own belief. To bring
about industrial competition, as, for instance, among the bidders at the sale of
a house, each one must know that his
desire to possess the building is opposed
by his competitors, who wish him not to
get it; and he will desire all the more to
get possession of it, if he knows that the
rest do not wish him to do so. Without
this, mere competition would be fruitless,

and political economists have erred here in not clearly distinguishing the special case where there exists, in the minds of the competitors, no knowledge at all of the competition, from the varying measure of that knowledge, as shown in the infinite number of degrees that separate complete understanding from complete ignorance of the fact.

This was my ground for saying, as I did further back, that the fundamental social opposition must be sought, not, as one might be tempted to think, at first sight, in the relation of two contrary or contradictory individuals, but rather in those logical and teleological duals, those curious combats between thesis and antithesis, between willing and *nilling*, whose stage is the consciousness of the social individual. Of course the question may be asked: If this be true, how does this social opposition differ from any purely psychological opposition? To this I reply: It differs in cause, and still more in effect.

First, as to its cause. When a solitary individual receives from his senses two apparently contradictory impressions, he hesitates between two sense judgments, one of which says that that spot down there is a lake, while the other denies it. Here is an internal opposition of purely psychological origin, a thing which occurs but seldom, however. Indeed, we may assert without fear of error that every doubt or hesitation experienced by even the most isolated man belonging to the most savage of tribes is due to an encounter within himself, either of two rays of instances which come together and interfere in his brain, or else of a single ray of instances which runs athwart of some sense perception. In writing, I often hesitate between two synonymous phrases, each of which appears preferable to the other under the given circumstances; here it is two rays of imitation that interfere within me — I refer to the two human series which, beginning with the first inventor of each of these phrases, have reached on down to myself. For, each of these phrases I learned from some individual, who learned it from some other, and so on up to the first one who uttered it. (This, let me say again, is what I mean by a *ray of imitation*, or imitative ray; and the sum total of rays of this kind derived from any single inventor, originator, or innovator, whose pattern is reproduced, is what I call an *imitative radiation*. Our social life includes a thick network of radiations of this sort, with countless mutual interferences.) Or, take other instances. Suppose I am a judge, and hesitate between a view based on a series of decrees following an opinion promulgated by some author, such as Marcadé or Demolombe, and an opposing view resting on another series of decrees emanating from some other commentator; this, again, is an interference of two imitative rays. Similarly, when I hesitate between gas and electricity as a means of illuminating my apartment. On the other hand, when a young peasant, observing the sunset, is at a loss whether to believe his schoolmaster, who assures him that the fall of night is due to the motion of the earth and not to the motion of the sun, or the testimony of his senses, which tell him the contrary, in such a case there is but a single imitative ray, which, reaching out through his schoolmaster, unites him with Galileo; nevertheless this is sufficient to render his hesitation, his own internal opposition, social in origin.

But it is above all in its effects, or rather in its lack of effectuality, that purely individual opposition differs from the fundamental form of social opposition, though the latter is individual also. Sometimes the individual's hesitation remains shut up within himself, and is neither reproduced nor tends to spread by imitation among his neighbors; in this case the phenomenon remains purely individual. But more often doubt itself is almost as contagious as faith, and any person who becomes sceptical in an environment that is fervent through force of example, is soon the source of a scepticism that radiates out from him and about him. Can we deny, in this case, the social character of the internal strife which each individual of this group experiences?

But let us face the question in a still more general way. When an individual becomes aware of a contradiction existing between one of his conclusions, aims, notions, or habits, — such as a dogma, turn of phraseology, commercial procedure, species of arm or tool, etc., — and the conclusion, aim, notion, or habit of some other man or men, one of three things happens. On the one hand, he may allow himself to be completely influenced by the other, and abruptly abandon his own mode of thinking or acting; in this case there is no internal strife, the victory occurs without a struggle, and presents one of the many instances of imitation which make up the social life. On the other hand, our individual may only half submit to the other's influence; this is the case we were considering above, and the shock is here followed by a diminution of its force, so that it becomes more or less weakened and paralyzed. Or, finally, he may actively oppose the strange action or habit, — the belief or volition with which he has come in contact, — and assert or desire all the more strenuously what he asserted and desired before. Yet, even in this last case, where he rouses all the strength of his conviction or passion to repel another's example, he experiences a certain unrest, an internal strife — though of another sort, it is true, and as inspiring as the former was enervating. This unrest, also, for the very reason that it results from an over-excitement and not a paralysis of one's individual force, is likely to spread contagiously; and this is what causes the splitting up of a society into parties. A new party always consists of a group of persons who, one after another and copying one another, have adopted a notion or course contrary to that which had hitherto reigned in their midst, and with which they themselves had been imbued. On the other hand, this new dogmatism, becoming more intense and intolerant as it spreads, raises against itself a coalition of those who, remaining faithful to tradition, have made exactly the opposite choice, and thus two fanatical parties find themselves face to face.

So we see that, whether in a violent, dogmatic form, or in a weaker, sceptical one, the juxtaposition of two opposite terms is social in character, provided it spreads by imitation. Were the case otherwise, we would be compelled to say that there is nothing social in such facts as these : the rivalry of two languages, as, for example, French and German, or

French and English, on their respective
frontiers, in Belgium, Switzerland, and
the Channel Islands; or the rivalry of
two religions which are neighbors. One
of these languages or religions constantly
encroaches on the other, as a result of
ceaseless battles waged, not between
rival human beings, but within each individual mind and consciousness, between
two rival phrases or faiths. Is there
anything that presents a greater sociological interest than these alluvial de-
posits of language and religion? Psychological oppositions, then, work themselves out in a social way, and it is always
proper to go back to that starting-point.
Nevertheless, it is quite important not
to confuse the two forms in which opposition presents itself, — the one, where the
struggle of the two juxtaposed terms
takes place in the individual himself, and
the other, where the individual adopts
but one of the opposing terms, although
the two are placed side by side within

him, and where, consequently, the struggle occurs only in his relations with other men. One may ask himself in this connection, as I asked long ago, in one of my first articles, [1] which is worse for a society: to be divided into parties and sects fighting over opposing programmes and dogmas, and into nations continually warring with one another, or to be composed of individuals at peace with one another, but each individually striving within himself, a prey to scepticism, irresolution, and discouragement? Is it better to enjoy this superficial peace, which covers up a state of fierce and ceaseless war in minds wrestling with themselves, or shall we admit that the bloodiest wars, even religious wars and the attacks of political fever which characterize the most blood-thirsty revolutions, are preferable to that torpor? Were it true that we must choose be-

[1] An article incorporated later into my *Laws of Imitation*, Ch. I, near the end.

tween these two solutions, it must be admitted that the social problem would be
exceedingly difficult to settle. And does
it not appear to be true ? Does it not
seem as though the moment men ceased
to make war upon one another on the
battlefield, or to fight one another des-
perately in the arena of industrial or
political competition, they fell into the
profound uneasiness characteristic of
anxious, vacillating, and discouraged souls,
wavering between priests and doctors
who contradict one another, between the
time-honored maxims of a lip-worshipped
ethics and the opposing practices of an
ethics that dares not as yet declare itself ?   And when men put an end to
their internal divisions, waverings and
discussions concerning opposing doc-
trines and lines of conduct, do they not
range themselves into two camps, according to the different choice they have
made, and proceed once more to fight
one another ?   We should have to choose,

then, between external war and internal strife. Such would seem to be the ultimate dilemma confronting those who dream of a perpetual peace, among whom I number myself.

Fortunately, the truth is not so sad and discouraging as they make out. Observation proves that every condition of strife, whether external or internal, always aims at, and ends by passing into, a decisive victory or a treaty of peace. As far as internal strife is concerned, whether we call it doubt, irresolution, anguish, or despair, one thing, at least, is evident : this sort of struggle always appears as an exceptional and transient crisis, and no one should take it upon himself to consider it the normal state of affairs or to judge it preferable (with all its painful agitations) to the so-called effeminate peace involving regular work under the guidance of a decided will and a securely formed judgment. And as regards external strife, the strug-

gle among men, can it be otherwise?
If history be correctly interpreted, it
shows that war is forever developing
in one particular direction, and that this
course, repeated hundreds of times and
easy to disentangle among the thickets
and undergrowth of history, seems to
indicate its ultimate disappearance, after
it has gradually become rarer.   In fact,
as a result of that imitative radiation,
which labors constantly and, so to speak,
clandestinely to enlarge the special field
of social phenomena, all the latter are
in process of enlargement, and war is
participating in the movement.   From
a countless number of very small but
exceedingly bitter wars between petty
clans, we pass to a smaller number of
somewhat larger and less rancorous wars:
first between small cities, then between
large cities, then between nations that
are continually growing greater, till
finally we arrive at an era of very
infrequent but most impressive conflicts,

quite devoid of hatred, between colossal nations, whose very greatness makes them inclined to peace.

Let me stop here to observe that, in thus passing from the small to the great, and from very numerous instances of the small to very rare cases of the great, the evolution of war, and of social phenomena generally, seems to contradict the evolution of the sciences as I have hitherto described it. Yet, as a matter of fact, it only serves as an indirect proof and confirmation. For since everything in the world of facts proceeds from small to great, everything in the world of ideas, which reflects it as though reversed in a mirror, naturally proceeds from great to small, and in the course of its analysis comes upon the elementary facts and real explanations only at the end of its journey.

To return now to the main discussion. At each of these successive stages and expansions, which are chiefly processes of tranquillization, war as a whole has dimin-

ished, or, at least, been transformed in
a manner tending toward its ultimate
disappearance. Each aggrandizement of
states, as they grew from tribes to cities,
and from cities to kingdoms, empires,
and immense federations, meant the sup-
pression of warfare in a region ever
more widely extended. There have always been on the earth, down to the
present day, certain regions, sometimes
quite limited, each of which was long regarded by its inhabitants as forming a
sort of universe by itself; for example,
a valley shut in by mountains, a large
island, a bit of continent nearly cut off
from the rest, and later on the entire
circumference of an inland sea. When
this miniature universe was pacified by
a series of conquests which put every
locality in it under the same yoke, it
seemed as if the final end sought for —
universal peace — were attained. Such a
momentary respite occurred in the empire of the Pharaohs, the Chinese Em-

pire, the Peru of the Incas, certain isles of the Pacific, and the Roman Empire. Unfortunately, no sooner was this fascinating goal dimly seen, than it fled farther away ; the earth appeared larger than had been suspected ; relations, first pacific, then belligerent, were set up with powerful neighbors, whose very existence had hitherto not been suspected ; these must be conquered or conquer, if the world's peace was to be firmly established. The development of war is, in fact, a gradual extension of the area of peace. But this extension cannot go on indefinitely ; this flitting mirage cannot forever torment our view, since the globe has limits and we have long since encircled it. What characterizes especially our own epoch and differentiates it widely, in a sense, from the entire past, although the laws of history apply to it no less nor more than to its predecessors, is this: that now, for the first time in history, the international polity of the great states of civilization

I

embraces within its purview, not merely
a single continent, or two at most, but
the whole globe, so that the last stage
of the evolution of war is at length discovering itself, in a vista so dazzling
that we can scarcely believe our eyes;
the end of this vista is certainly difficult
to attain, but it is a real end, and no
deception this time, and it can no longer
move away as we approach it. Is
there not something in this fitted to in-
spire every heart? After establishing
peace on the borders of a river, such
as the Nile or the Amur, and on the
coasts of a small sea, — after playing first
a fluvial and then a Mediterranean rôle,
as Metchnikoff has pointed out, and as
the laws of imitative radiation explain to
perfection, — civilization is in a fair way
to become oceanic, that is to say, world-
wide; and the critical period of growth
being now past, the grand harvest season
is about to begin.

It is, of course, true that when war is

at an end the painful struggles among mankind will not be found to have disappeared entirely. There are other forms of strife besides war, notably competition. But what has just been said applies also to competition, which is a social opposition of the economic instead of the political type. Like war, competition proceeds from the small to the great, and from very numerous instances of the very small to very infrequent instances of the very great. Ever since its inception, competition has appeared in three forms: as among the producers of the same article, as among the consumers of the same article, and between producer and consumer or seller and buyer of the same article. For, as respects different articles, there is no mutual opposition of desires; there is, rather, a mutual adaptation, when the articles in question are capable of being exchanged.

Since we touch here on a very delicate question, which can be approached

for the present only from a special side,
and without joining either the party of col-
lectivists or their opponents, let us make
one or two remarks, whose truth is not
open to question. *Competition* is an am-
biguous word which signifies at once, or
in turn, *joint action* and *contest*,[1] and this
is why a dispute goes on incessantly
between those who, seeing only the opposition aspect of this equivocal phenomenon, rightly deprecate it, and those who,
regarding it only from the adaptation
side, laud it for the civilizing inventions
it has brought about. However, it is
only the unfavorable side that we are
considering here.

It is not at all essential that the desires of the different consumers or the different producers of the same article should
conflict or contradict one another; not

[1] The English word *competition* leans decidedly to
the latter meaning; the French word *concurrence*, which
the author uses, means both competition and concurrent
action. — Tr.

even when the desires of some are con-
fronted with the desires of others. The
producer and the buyer are always in
accord to this extent, that one wishes to
buy what the other wishes to sell; true,
it is not always at the same price, but
there is always some price that brings
them into agreement and ends the dispute between them. Nor are the desires
of the producers in any respect contradictory, so long as each has his own particular patronage and market, inextensible
for the time being, like his production;
they come into conflict only when, with
the extension of the facilities of production, each desires to produce more, and
to appropriate to his own advantage the
production of others. It is true that, as
civilization results in a constant growth
of the power of production, this strife
between co-producers is inevitable and
bound to become constantly more severe.
Finally, as regards the desires of the
consumers of a given article, we may

say that, far from being mutually injurious, the competitors for the purchase of an article more frequently aid one another, when the production of that article is of such a character as to proceed *pari passu* with its consumption : thus, the more people there are who wish to purchase bicycles, the more the price of bicycles will fall. The desires of the consumers are really contradictory only in case the supply of the article in question is less than the demands for it, as frequently happens with the prime necessities of life and also the greatest luxuries — and in case the supply cannot be increased as rapidly as the desire for it increases through the contagious influence of fashion.

To return to our previous discussion, after making these explanations, it should be observed that each of the three kinds of competition here distinguished obeys the law already pointed out. As between buyer and seller, the petty bargainings of the small markets of primitive times were ceaseless and innumerable. Gradually these are done away with, but only to be replaced by those greater sales to which the imposition by the municipal councils of a municipal tax on wheat or meat gives rise. When these are abolished in turn, they are replaced by still greater transactions, and by discussions in parliament concerning measures which aim to promote the interests of the mass of producers or the mass of consumers in the nation, by imposing or abolishing certain customs duties. The so-called consumers' coöperative societies, that is, societies in which the consumer and producer are one, are born of the desire to put an end to this species of competition and they develop with the latter. Among purchasers, the competition goes on increasing also.[1]   In small primitive

---

[1] In times of famine, to-day, there is not a sack of flour in the remotest village of the Crimea or America that does not find as competitors for its possession, not

markets the competition for a sack of flour or head of cattle is limited to a few persons. When these markets begin to extend and diminish in number, these countless little competitions end either in an amalgamation of interests, or too often in little local monopolies, and are succeeded by more extensive competitions, that grow constantly more extensive, till they also culminate either in important unions, such as the agricultural syndicates, or in vaster monopolies, such as the gigantic *kartells* or trusts with which we are all familiar.

But let us turn to the form of competition which has been most studied, and which is in reality the fiercest, because it

merely a few persons in the neighborhood, as formerly, but the merchants of all the European nations. Similarly, in ordinary times, there is not a masterpiece of art, nor an old book in the most obscure of French castles, that does not have to fear a contest for its purchase, not merely among a few amateurs of the neighborhood or province or of all France, but even among the billionnaires of America.

is the most clearly perceived ; namely, that between producers.   It begins with count-less rivalries among petty merchants who contend over miniature markets, originally side by side, yet almost without com-munication.   But as the latter, breaking down their barriers, pass over into greater but less numerous markets, the petty rival shops also consolidate, either voluntarily or perforce, into greater but less numerous factories, in which the work of production, hitherto a prey to its own jealous opposi-tion, is now harmoniously coördinated ; and the rivalry of these factories repro-duces, on a larger scale, the former rivalry of the shops, until, with the gradual ex-pansion of the markets, which tend to become a single market, we arrive at a stage where there remain merely a few giants of industry and commerce, which are still rivals, unless, indeed, they also have come to some understanding.

In short, competition develops in con-centric circles, which are continually en-

larging.   But the underlying condition and
raison d'être of this enlargement of competition is the enlargement of association.
Of association *or monopoly*, our opponents
will insist.   Granted; yet monopoly is but
one of two solutions which the problem of
competition admits, just as imperial unity
is but one of two solutions to the problem
of war.   The former problem may be
solved by association of individuals, as the
latter is capable of solution by a federation
of peoples.   Moreover, monopoly itself, as
it extends, becomes alleviated, and if, in
certain kinds of production, it should become universal, — the goal toward which
it is tending, and which M. Paul Leroy-
Beaulieu is, I believe, wrong in considering
absolutely and forever unattainable,[1] —

[1] A monopoly is always partial and relative. Undoubtedly M. Paul Leroy-Beaulieu is right in saying
that competition never results in an *absolute* and *complete*
monopoly ; and the instance he cites of the great stores,
the Bon Marché, for example, which, after overcoming
the competition of so many little stores, has experienced
new competition from the Louvre, the Printemps, the

it would probably be more bearable, often times, than the condition of acute competition whose place it takes. Competition, then, tends either to monopoly (at least a partial and relative one) or to the association of competitors, just as war leads to a crushing of the vanquished, or to the conclusion of a fair treaty with him — in either case, to at least a partial and rela-

Samaritaine, etc., seems at first sight convincing. But in reality, *within a certain radius* and *to a certain extent,* each of these colossi of commerce has succeeded in monopolizing a field for which thousands of petty firms were contending; each has its own particular following in the country — a following which, for some reason or other, whether caprice or fashion, belongs exclusively to itself. This is, most frequently, merely for the reason that it has the reputation of excelling its rivals in the quality of *some particular article.* Really, this so-called competition between great stores can easily be moderated and toned down by mutual understandings, which are far more easy to reach, on account of the small number interested, than in the case of the more numerous smaller firms whose place they take ; and, furthermore, such competition tends more and more to become a mere division of labor, or rather an apportionment of partial monopolies which they have come to share or are gradually beginning to share.

tive pacification.   The growth of conquering states led to this same result.   The great modern states, taking the place of the mediæval fiefs, inaugurated a reign of peace which has hitherto, I admit, been incomplete and brief, but which is increasing in extent and duration, like the great armaments of the present day.   To deny that competition passes over into monopoly (or into association), and to believe that we are thereby defending competition against those who decry it, is simply to reject the one excuse that can be put forward in its favor.   It is just as though, in order to defend militarism against the attacks that have been made upon it, we strove to demonstrate that war did not bring peace in its train, as a consequence of victory.   War, it is true, only passes over into peace that it may spring to life again, out of peace, on a far grander scale ; and so, too, competition only resolves itself temporarily into association that it may reappear again, out of association, in the form of rivalries between associations, corporations, syndicates, and so on. But in this way we finally arrive at a certain limited number of gigantic associations which, not being open to further growth, can only associate together, after having fought one another awhile.

A third great form of social strife is *discussion*. This is doubtless implied in the preceding ; but, if war and competition are discussions, one is a discussion in deeds of blood, the other a discussion in deeds of ruin. Let us say a word now with regard to verbal discussion, pure and simple. This, too, when it develops, — for there are any number of little private discussions which, fortunately, do not develop, but die on the spot, — develops in the way just described, though here the process is far less obvious. It is only after the mental discussion between contradictory ideas within the same mind has ended (this should not be forgotten), that any verbal discussion is possible between two men who have solved the question differently. Similarly, if verbal, written, or printed discussions between groups of men, and groups that are ever widening, takes the place of verbal discussion between two men, it is because the more limited discussion has been brought to an end by some relative and temporary agreement, or some sort of unanimity. These groups are first split up into an endless multitude of little coteries, clans, churches, forums, and schools, which combat one another; but at length, after many polemics, they are welded into a very small number of great parties, religions, parliamentary groups, schools of philosophy, and schools of art, which engage one another in mortal combat. Was it not thus that the Catholic faith became gradually established? In the first two or three centuries of the Church's history, countless discussions, always intense and often bloody, were waged among the members of each local church, ending in their agreeing upon a creed; but this creed, disagreeing in certain particulars with those

of neighboring churches, gave rise to con-
ferences and provincial councils, which
solved the difficulties, excepting that they
occasionally disagreed with one another,
and were forced to carry their disputes
higher up, to national or œcumenical councils. The political unity of ancient
France, under a monarchical form of government, was similarly brought about; and
the political unity of modern France, along
democratic lines, is in process of construction in the same way. What I may call
linguistic unity (that is, the unity of national language, which succeeds rivalries
among dialects and provincialisms that re-
sist the purifying tendency) has been similarly established. The unity of legal codes
has long since been accomplished in an
analogous manner: countless local customs
have arisen, settling thousands of individual discussions concerning rights (though
not all, as the court records prove); these
customs, coming into conflict with one another, have been reconciled by certain

sectional customs, which have finally been replaced by uniform legislation. The unity of science, operating slowly over a wide field, through a succession of discussions, alternately settled and reopened, among scientists and scientific schools, would give rise to similar reflections.

Among these various forms of discussion, one in particular deserves attention, namely, judicial discussion or the trial of civil suits. Is it true that the scope of judicial procedure is likewise enlarging, and by this very growth is rushing to its own extinction? However strange this proposition may appear at first, it is certainly true. In the first place, it is clear that, among primitive peoples, trials were in no way different from private wars; in fact, except for the presence of the sovereign judge, the state, most of the differences between litigants would have ended in blows. Trials are modified duels; they are wars in embryo. And, conversely, wars are

law-suits between nations; they are a
litigation that has attained its natural
development, through the absence of any
supra-national authority. If, then, we
compare the judicial contests of to-day
that occur before tribunals, with those of
the Middle Ages, where the parties concerned were armed champions, or with
the earlier ones between kindred tribes,
we must acknowledge that the heat of
litigation has continually grown less.
And I may add that it has grown less
by reason of these very extensions. In
fact, we may say that the scope of legal
questions has been extended, as local
customs gave place to provincial customs,
and finally to national laws; at each step
in the process of judicial unification,
every kind of law-suit (that is, every
question of right) leads to two diamet-
rically opposite opinions, and thus becomes more general in character. Now
it is through just such a process of gen-
eralization that every kind of discussion

K

finally arrives at its last stage : a deci-
sion of the Supreme Court, which dries
up the fountain-head of this species of
suit. How many fountain-heads of this
sort have been dried up, even within the
present century !

The objection may possibly be raised
that as races become more civilized they
tend more and more to discussion, and
that, far from taking the place of private
discussion, our public discussions, polemics of the press, and parliamentary
debates only add fuel to them. But
such an objection would be without
force. For if savages and barbarians
discuss little (which is fortunate, since
most of their discussions degenerate into
quarrels and combats), it is because they
scarcely speak or think at all. When
we consider the very small number of
their ideas, we ought to be surprised
that they clash so often, relatively
speaking ; and we should marvel to
find men with so few different interests

so quarrelsome. On the other hand, a thing which we ought to wonder at, but which we scarcely notice, as a matter of fact, is this: that in our own civilized cities, despite the great current of ideas sweeping over us in conversation and reading, there are, on the whole, so few discussions, and these so lacking in warmth. We should be amazed to find that men who think and talk so much contradict one another so seldom, to see that they accomplish so much and clash so little; just as we should wonder at seeing so few carriage accidents in our streets, which are so animated and crowded, or at seeing so few wars break out in this era of complex and far-reaching international relations. What is it, then, that has brought us into agreement on so many points? It is the three great productions, that have been gradually wrought out by centuries of discussion, namely, Religion, Jurisprudence, and Science. We may note, also, that in a civilized country public discussions far exceed private ones in importance, lively interest, and earnestness, even, while in a barbarous land the reverse is true. Our parliamentary sessions are increasing in violence, while the tone of discussions in the café and the drawing-room is softening.[1]

To sum up. The strife of opposition in human society, in its three principal forms — war, competition, and discussion — proves obedient to one and the same law of development, through ever widening areas of temporary pacification, alternating with renewals of discord more centrally organized and on a larger scale, and leading up to a final, at least partial, agreement. It would appear from this — and we have many other reasons for the conclusion — that the strife of opposition fulfils the rôle of a middle term

[1] The reader may be reminded of Bagehot's treatment of "The Age of Discussion" in his *Physics and Politics.* — Ed.

in the social, as it does in the organic
and inorganic, worlds, and that it is
destined gradually to fade away, exhaust
itself, and disappear, as a result of its
own growth, which is merely a progress
toward its own destruction.

Indeed, it is now a favorable moment
for stating, or rather restating more explicitly, the relation between those three
great scientific aspects of the universe
which I call the Repetition, Opposition,
and Adaptation of phenomena. The
last two arise out of the first, and the
second is usually, though not always,
an intermediary between the first and
third. It is because physical forces
spread, or tend to spread, in a geometrical ratio, by their own wave-like repetitions, that they interfere, or, on the other
hand, combine adaptively; their *shocks*
of interference apparently serve only as
preparations for their *unions* of interference, that is, their combinations. It is
because living species tend to increase

in a geometrical ratio by the hereditary repetition of individual copies, that they interfere, and give rise, either to felicitous and fruitful cross-breeds or to the struggles for existence so carefully studied by the Darwinians, who regard vital interference only from its sanguinary side, considering it, with obvious exaggeration, as the sole or chief factor in the creation of new species, that is, in the readaptation of old species. And, similarly, it is because certain social phenomena, such as a dogma, phrase, scientific principle, moral maxim, prayer, industrial process, or the like, tend to spread in a geometrical ratio by imitative repetition, that they interfere with one another in a felicitous or infelicitous manner. That is, the discordant sides of their nature come together in certain minds, giving rise to logical or teleological duels, which constitute first germs of social oppositions (wars, competitions, and polemics); while the harmonious sides of their nature come together in the mind of the genius, or sometimes even in the ordinary mind, producing true logical syntheses, inventions, and fruitful originations, which are the source of all social adaptation.

These three terms constitute a circular series which is capable of proceeding on and on without ceasing. It is through imitative repetition that invention, the fundamental social adaptation, spreads and is strengthened, and tends, through the encounter of one of its own imitative rays with an imitative ray emanating from some other invention, old or new, either to arouse new struggles, or (perhaps directly, perhaps as a result of these struggles) to yield new and more complex inventions, which soon radiate out imitatively in turn, and so on indefinitely. Observe that the logical *duel*, the fundamental term in the social struggle of opposition, like logical *synthesis*, the fundamental term in social adaptation, requires repetition in order to become social, to become generalized, and grow. But with this difference: the imitative spread of the internal condition of discord between two ideas, or even of the external state of discord between two men, one of whom has chosen one of these ideas and the other the other, is bound to use up and put an end to this discord in the course of time, since every combat is exhausting and results in some victory; whereas the imitative spread of the state of harmony, whether internal or external, which finds expression in the lighting up of a new beacon of truth, is a synthesis of our previous knowledge, or a communion between our minds and all other minds that see its beams, and hence has no reason to be arrested, but rather becomes strengthened as it advances. Thus, of the three terms compared, the first and third far surpass the second in height, depth, importance, and possibly also duration. The only value of the second — opposition — is to provoke a tension of antagonistic forces fitted to arouse inventive genius; such is a military invention which, by placing victory in one camp, temporarily ends war; an industrial invention which, hav, ing been adopted or monopolized by some one among the various industrial rivals, insures his triumph, and temporarily puts an end to competition; or some philosophical, scientific, legal, or æsthetic invention, which suddenly puts an end to countless discussions, though at the risk of giving birth to new ones later on. This is the sole value of opposition, its only *raison d'être*. Yet how often does the invention that it calls for fail to respond! How often does war cut down genius, instead of raising it up! How many talents are rendered worthless by the polemics of the press, parliamentary debates, or even the foolish fencings of congresses and associations! All that we can say — and this supports the conclusions above reached — is that the historic order of succession in preponderance, among the three forms of struggle mentioned, is precisely the order of their fitness to stimulate inventiveness. Thus man has passed from an era where war was dominant to a phase where competition predominated, and finally to an age of discussion. Moreover, as society becomes civilized, exchange develops faster than competition, conversation faster than discussion, and internationalism faster than militarism.

We have thus far spoken only of the *strife* oppositions, that is, the oppositions that occur between simultaneous terms which collide. As regards *rhythmic* oppositions, which consist of successive terms, — whether qualities or quantities it matters not, — such as an alternate rise and fall, come and go, etc., it would seem at first sight as if these were less enigmatic than the former, inasmuch as they do not involve any paralysis and mutual destruction of forces. But, looking at the matter more closely, we see that this come and go of forces, which act in turn for and against, or pronounce alternately a *yes* and a *no*, is even more difficult to understand than the interaction of two forces that collide and then come to an equilibrium. The destructive interferences present at least an appearance of accident and unexpectedness, and we know them to be scarcely separable from creative interferences, such as the shadow of the body; not to mention the fact that the equilibration or mutual neutralization of opposite tendencies in us, including those due to rival suggestions from without, permit our natural characteristics to come to light, which is perhaps one of the best justifications of the phenomenon of strife. But rhythm appears to be a normal play of forces which voluntarily accommodate themselves to one another, whether it be in qualitative or quantitative rhythm. Indeed, I admit that I would be filled with a Schopenhauerian despair, were there

serious grounds for supposing that this
come and go, this childish see-sawing
back and forth, held true on a large scale,
that the process of dissolution was the
exact inverse of evolution, regression the
inverse of progress, and that everything
proceeded forthwith to begin over again,
indefinitely, without any resulting coördination.   Fortunately, this is not the case;
for rhythm, that regular and somewhat
exact rhythm which alone is worthy of
the name, appears only in the details of
phenomena, as a condition of their exact
repetition, and through this of their
variation.   The orbit of a heavenly body
repeats itself only by reason of its passing to and fro in an ellipse; similarly, a
sound-wave or a light-wave repeats itself
only by reason of its rectilinear or circular
or elliptical path to and fro; the contrac-
tion of a muscular element and the inner-
vation of a nervous element are propa-
gated in the muscle or along the nerve
only by means of a minute circular process

which·returns again to its own starting-
point; and Baldwin has recently shown
that imitation itself is a "circular reaction," and that it may be defined as a
"brain-state due to stimulating conditions,
muscular reaction which reproduces or
retains the stimulating conditions, same
brain-state again due to same stimulating conditions, and so on." In the
work from which this quotation is taken,
he extends the meaning of the word
imitation far beyond that which I assigned it; and, generalizing the term in
such a way as to include both the vital
and the social functions, he writes : " The
self-repeating or circular type of reaction,
to which the name imitation is given . . .
is seen to be fundamental and to remain
the same, as far as structure is concerned,
for all motor activity whatever." But
repetition, the regular, rhythmic succession
of phenomena, is only the underlying
condition of their course and evolution,
which is always more or less irregular

and picturesque, and becomes more so as it progresses. Now, rhythmic outgo and return exhibits some exactness, it is true, but only in its order of succession, not in its course. This is the case even with quantitative rhythm, including those general instances of rise and fall that statistics finds a means of measuring along the path of a civilization in process of development. It is exceedingly seldom that the increase and decrease observed here are equal and similar; for instance, that the ascending curves representing wealth, the price of securities on exchange, religious faith, education, criminality, etc., are found to be oppositely reflected in descending curves, presenting the same general and special characteristics. This is well known to statisticians. I have myself noted elsewhere the irreversible character of a host of social evolutions, which are the most important of any. I need not return to that question here.

We conclude, then, that opposition, in

its two great forms, reveals and accentu-
ates ever more clearly its own auxiliary
and intermediate character. As rhythm,
it is only of direct service to repetition,
and of indirect service to variation, and
it disappears when the latter appears.
As strife, it is only of use in stimulating
adaptation, with which we may now proceed to deal.

CHAPTER III

THE ADAPTATION OF PHENOMENA

THE explanations given in the two preceding chapters have already prepared us to understand the real meaning of the word *adaptation*, which expresses the profoundest aspect under which science views the universe. Here, again, we shall see that the evolution of science, in any field of truth whatsoever, consists in a passage from the great to the small, from the vague to the exact, and from the false or superficial to the true and deep-rooted; that is, it consists in first discovering or imagining a vast harmony of the whole, or a few grand but vague external harmonies, and in replacing these gradually by countless internal harmonies, forming an infinite number of fruitful, infinitesimal adaptations. We shall observe, also, that the evolution of reality, which is, here as elsewhere, exactly the reverse of that of thought about it, consists in a ceaseless tendency on the part of minute internal harmonies to externalize and enlarge themselves more and more. Incidentally, we cannot help noticing, as has been already noted, that, while the progress of knowledge enables us to discover new and deeper harmonies, it also reveals many deeper and hitherto unobserved incongruities.

But we must begin first with a few definitions or necessary explanations. What is, precisely, an adaptation, or natural harmony? Let us take an example outside of life, where the teleological connection between the organ and its function is so obvious as not to require explanation. Suppose we choose the basin of a river. Here we find a mountain

L

or a chain of hills *adapted* to the down-
flow of the river's waters, and the sun-
beams adapted to the uplifting of the
ocean's waters to the clouds; further,
the winds are adapted to transporting
these clouds to the mountain summits,
where they fall again in showers and
supply the springs, brooks, and rivers
which are tributary to the one great
water-course. Thus we find here an
unstable equilibrium, a circuit of acts
that are interlaced and repeat themselves
with variations. A living being, we may
say, forms a similar circuit, only a much
more complex one; and, moreover, the
adaptation in him is not one-sided, as in
the instance cited, but reciprocal. The
organ serves to fulfil a vital function, and reciprocally the vital function
serves to maintain the organ; whereas, in
the case of the streams upon our planet,
the mountain is adapted to the flow of the
waters; but the flow of waters, far from
effecting the preservation of the mountain,

has the effect of denuding it, and gradually carrying it away. And so, too, there is no reciprocity in the adaptation of the sun's heat to the irrigation of the soil.

It is always, remember, a harmony that is repeated; we have observed it already, let us point out other instances. Every planet of the solar system, considered mechanically, that is, considered as a moving point, reveals a harmony between its inclination to fall into the sun and its tendency to fly away at a tangent; this would constitute an opposition, if these two forces, the centripetal and centrifugal, tended to exert themselves along the same straight line; but since they act at right angles to each other, adaptation ensues. (In this way opposition and adaptation are transformed, one into the other, in nature.)[1] Now the

[1] A waterspout or cyclone is likewise an atmospheric harmony, a circuit of acts due to the interworking of two forces which do not impede, but reënforce each other in their resultant.

planet's orbit is a repetition, the *varied* repetition, of this mechanical adaptation. Again, considered geologically, from the standpoint of its stratigraphic and physico-chemical composition, a planet is a most harmonious adjustment of superimposed strata; and, if we may believe M. Stanislas Meunier on this point, the same adjustment occurs in every planet and in the general constitution of the solar system itself. An imaginary cross-section of the earth, from centre to circumference, would give a succession of incandescent layers, followed by solid layers, then liquid, then gaseous, each essential to the succeeding one; and this order of succession corresponds to the natures of the planets that we find if we start from the sun as centre and go toward the limits of the system, to Neptune, which is gaseous. However, the truth of this analogy is of little importance.

Any aggregation whatsoever is a collection of individuals jointly adapted,

either some adapted to the remainder
or all to a common function. An aggregate means an *adaptate*. Moreover, different aggregates which have relations
with one another may be coadapted;
this constitutes an *adaptate* of a higher
degree, and an infinite number of such
degrees may be distinguished. For the
sake of simplicity, let us distinguish
merely between two degrees of adaptation : adaptation of the first degree is
that which the elements of the system
in question have among themselves; adaptation of the second degree is that
which unites these elements to the systems that surround them, that is, to
what is vaguely denoted by the term *environment*. The adjustment with one's self
differs greatly, in phenomena of every sort,
from the adjustment with others, just as
self-repetition (habit) differs from the
repetition of others (heredity or imitation), and as self-opposition (hesitation
and doubt) differs from opposition to

others (strife or competition.) Often
these two kinds of opposition are to a
certain extent mutually exclusive. Thus
in the matter of political organizations,
it has frequently been observed that the
most self-consistent — those that are the
most logically deduced and that present in
the highest degree the characteristics of
adaptation — are least adapted to meet
the requirements of their inherited and
natural environment; and, conversely, that
the most practical are the least logical.
The same remark applies to grammars,
religions, the fine arts, etc.; thus the one
perfect grammar, the only one whose rules
are quite without exception, is the grammar
of — Volapük! It applies to organisms
as well; there are some that are so perfect as to be almost incapable of living, and
that would be better fitted for life if they
were less perfect; for perfectness of accom-
modation may detract from suppleness.[1]

[1] A mental intuition or idea being given, the intellectual progress starting from this idea (which is usually

These preliminaries settled, let us point out the truth of the two propositions which were stated above. The partisans of final causes have done their best to discredit the notion of finality. It is nevertheless true that the first babblings of science date from the moment when this notion was introduced, even in its mystical and least rational form, into our representation of the world. What did primitive consciousness imagine, as it looked upon the universe of stars? It imagined a single, vast, fanciful adaptation, born of the so-called geocen-

a mixture of truth and error) may proceed in two different directions: first, in the direction of an adaptation of the first degree merely, that is, a gradual harmonizing of that idea with itself, along the line of differentiation and self-consistency. This is the course taken by many systems of philosophy and of metaphysics. Second, in the direction of an adaptation of the second degree, that is, a gradual harmonizing of that idea with the material received through the senses, and with the external data supplied by perception and discovery generally. This is the course taken by science. In the first case the advance often consists in passing from a lesser to a greater error.

tric illusion; all the stars (it thought) existed for the sake of the earth; the earth, and within the earth a single city or castle, were considered to be the focal point of the whole firmament, and the latter was supposed to be busying itself solely and unceasingly with ephemeral creatures like ourselves. Astrology was the logical outcome of this magnificent but imaginary adaptation of the sky to the earth and man. The true astronomy not only abolished this absurd harmony, but shattered the unity of the celestial harmony as well, breaking it up into as many partial harmonies as there are solar systems; the latter prove to be coherent and symmetrically coördinated as individuals, but bound together by exceedingly vague and doubtful bonds, being grouped in shapeless nebulæ and scattered constellations, presenting a sparkling disorder. Though the human reason takes greater delight in order than in anything else, it must nevertheless aban-

don its attempt to discover the clearest
marks of divine coördination in that all-
embracing world-group, the Cosmos, the
object of man's deepest admiration. To
find such marks, we must descend to the
solar system, and there, as we come to
know this little universe better, it is the
details, rather than the general effect of
this exquisite grouping of masses, that
arouses our delight. The relations of the
planets to one another do not strike us
with as much astonishment as the relation
of each planet to its satellites, and still
more the geological formations on the
surface of each sphere, the arrangement
of its water-courses, and its chemical
composition, all of which reveal so exact
an agreement. Henceforth, the religious
mind need turn no longer far away to
the vast vault of heaven, there to find
and worship the fathomless wisdom that
moves the universe; rather, it must gaze
into the chemist's crucible, and there
discern the mystery of those physical

harmonies that are surely the most exact
and marvellous of all — far more wonderful even than the scattered disorder
of the stars : I mean the chemical combinations. If, by means of some powerful microscope, we could perceive the
interior of a molecule, how much more
fascinating after all would appear the
great network of elliptical and circular
motions that in all probability make it
up, than the extremely simple play of the
great celestial tops !

If we pass from the physical world
to the world of life, there, too, we find
that the first step of reason was to
formulate the notion of a single grand
adaptation — the adaptation of the whole
organic creation, both vegetable and animal, to the ends of humanity, for its
nourishment, amusement, or protection, or
to warn it of secret dangers. Augury
and totemism, which are found among
all peoples in the beginning, originate
in this. However much the growth of

knowledge has dissipated this anthropo-
centric illusion, something of it still remained in that erroneous view, so long
accepted by natural philosophers, which
consisted in representing the palæonto-
logical series as a straight ascent toward
man, and in regarding every species,
whether extinct or living, as one chord
in a grand concert called the Divine
Plan of Nature — an ideal and regular
structure, with man at the top. Pain-
fully, and by dint of denials accumulated by observation, mankind was led
to give up this cherished idea; then it
was recognized that Nature does not exert
her wonderful harmonizing power to the
greatest degree along the broad lines of
the evolution of beings, — a ramified and
tortuous path, — nor yet in the grouping
of these different species into zonal flora
and fauna (though remarkable adaptation
is exhibited in *commensalism*, or the relations of insects with the flowers of
certain plants); but that it is exerted,

rather, in the details of each organism.
The partisans of final causes have, I
believe, diminished the value of the notion by making an erroneous and im-
proper use of it, though not an excessive one, for, on the contrary, I should
reproach them with having made much
too restricted a use of it, through their
unifying turn of mind. There is no
single end in nature — no end in relation to which all others are means;
but there is an infinite number of ends
which are seeking to utilize one another.
Every organism, and in every organism
every cell, and in every cell, perhaps,
every cellular element, has its own particular Providence, for itself and in itself.
Here, then, as before, we are led to
consider the harmonizing force (certainly
that which positive science has a right
to consider, without, however, denying
the possibility of some other), not as
something unique, external, and superior,
but as indefinitely repeated, infinitesimal,

and internal. In reality, the source of all these harmonies of life, which become less striking the farther we get from the starting-point and the wider the field we embrace, is the fertilized germ; this last is a living representation of the intersecting lines that meet in it, forming often a felicitous cross-breed; it is the germ of new talents, which are destined to spread broadcast and propagate themselves in turn, thanks to the survival of the fittest, or the elimination of the least fit.

Let us pass, now, to the social world. The theologians, who have ever been the most prominent sociologists, though without knowing that they were sociologists, frequently picture the stream of the history of all peoples of the earth as converging, from the beginnings of humanity, toward the advent of their own cult. On this point see Bossuet. In vain has sociology endeavored to secularize itself; it has never wholly freed itself from this sort of presupposition. Comte brought over in a masterly way the thoughts of Bossuet, whom he admired, with reason; with him, the entire history of mankind converged toward the era of his own Positivism, which thus became a species of secular neo-Catholicism. In the eyes of Augustin Thierry, Guizot, and other philosophers of history who flourished about 1830, the whole course of European history appeared to converge toward — the July Monarchy! Certainly it is not sociology that Comte founded; however admirably carried out, it is merely a *philosophy of history* that he offers us under this title, and it is the last word of the philosophy of history. Like all the systems that have been designated by that name, his conception unwinds human history before our eyes like a twisted skein; or rather it is a confused mass of many-colored skeins; it appears under the guise of a single development, the sole production of a sort of unique trilogy or tragedy, constructed according to the rules of its kind — where everything is bound together, where each of the three interlocked pieces is composed of phases linked to one another, each link being adapted to and riveted exclusively to the succeeding, and where the whole moves irresistibly on toward the final climax.

Spencer has made a great step in the direction of a healthier understanding of social adaptation; his formula of social evolution applies, not to a single drama, but to a considerable number of different social dramas. The evolutionists of his school, in thus formulating the laws of linguistic, religious, economic, political, moral, and æsthetic development, understand, at least implicitly, that these laws are capable of governing, not merely the single succession of peoples whose privilege it is to be called historic, but equally well all peoples that have existed or are to exist in future.

But still, in a multitude of forms, though on a smaller scale, the same error always comes to light, namely, the error of believing that, in order to see a gradual dawn of regularity, order, and logic in social phenomena, we must go outside of the details, which are essentially irregular, and rise high enough to obtain a panoramic view of the general effect; that the source and foundation of every social coördination is some general fact from which it descends gradually to particular facts, though always diminishing in strength; in short, that man acts, but a law of evolution guides him.

I hold the contrary, in a certain sense. Not that I deny the existence of certain slopes common to the diverse and multiform historical evolutions of races, which flow like rivers into the same basin; and I am well aware that, while many of these brooks and rivers are lost *en route*, others, flowing together, one after another, through a thousand eddies, end by mingling in one general current, which, in spite of its division into different branches, does not seem likely, in future, to empty out through several different mouths. But I see, too, that the real cause of this vast river, the final outcome of these various streams, in other words, of this final preponderance of a single line of social evolution (that of the so-called historic races), is the series of scientific discoveries and industrial inventions that have gone on ceaselessly accumulating and making use of one another ; these have become bound together in a system or bundle, whose real logical interrelation, though not without intricacies of its own, seems vaguely repeated in the interrelation of the races which have contributed to its formation. If we follow up this great scientific and industrial stream, we find its source in the mind of every genius, whether obscure or celebrated, who has added some new truth, some new means of activity, to the enduring legacy of humanity, and who has made the relations

M

among mankind more harmonious by this contribution, by promoting community of thought and collaboration of effort. And so, in opposition to the philosophers of whom I have been speaking, I maintain that the details of human events alone contain striking adaptations; that the basis of those harmonies which are less noticeable in a vaster domain here comes plainly to view, and that the more we rise from a small but closely united social group, such as the family, the school, the workshop, the rural church, the convent, or the regiment, to the city, the province, or the nation, the less complete and striking does this solidarity become. So, too, there is generally more logic in a phrase than in a discourse, and more in a single discourse than in a succession or group of discourses; there is more in one special rite than in a whole religion, in one point of law than in a whole legal code, in one particular scientific theory than in the whole body of science; and there is more in a single piece of work executed by one workman than in the sum total of his performances.

This is true, be it observed, unless some powerful personality intervenes to govern and overrule the interrelation of events. The latter, however, tends to occur more and more frequently, since civilization is distinguished by the facilities it offers for the realization of special schemes of social reorganization; and in this case it does not always hold true that the harmony of an aggregate is in inverse ratio to its mass. Often, indeed, the greater mass may be the more harmonious, and this occurs more and more frequently. For instance, the French administrative system, organized by the despotic genius of Napoleon, is quite as well adapted to its own *general* end as any of the least of its wheels is to its own *particular* end. The Prussian system of state railways is as well adapted to its higher strategic end as any of its stations can possibly be to its own commercial or other ends. The systems of Kant, Hegel, and Spencer are all as consistent in their general coördination as any of the little partial theories that serve as their material. A well-codified scheme of legislation may exhibit as much order in the arrangement of its sections and chapters as any of the partial laws that it embodies presents in its various interrelations. Finally, when a religion has been moulded into an aggressive theology, the concatenation of its dogmas may be, or appear to be, more logical than each of them taken separately. Yet, as is easy to see, these facts, though apparently contrary to those formulated above, really vie with them in demonstrating that the individual mind is the source of all social harmony. For these excellent coördinations must have been conceived long before they could be executed; they existed in the form of an idea hidden in a few cerebral cells, long before they began to cover so wide a domain.

Shall we not say, then, that the *funda-mental social adaptation* is, in the last analysis, that of two men, one of whom answers, by word or deed, the question of the other, whether silent, spoken, or tacit? I call it a "question," for the satisfaction of a need, like the solution of a problem, is the answer to a question. Shall we not say, then, that this fundamental harmony consists in the relation between two men, one of whom teaches, while the other learns — one of whom commands, while the other obeys — one of whom produces, while the other buys and consumes — one of whom is actor, poet, or artist, while the other is spectator, reader, or amateur; or, better, that it consists in the relation between two who work together to produce the same result? Certainly; for this relation, though it *implies* the relationship of two men, one of whom is pattern, the other copy, is really quite distinct from it.

In my judgment, however, we must

carry the analysis still farther, and, as I have already intimated, seek the fundamental social adaptation in the brain and individual mind of the inventor. Invention, if we limit the term to that which is destined to be imitated (for what remains locked up in the mind of its creator, has no social value),—invention, I say, is a harmony among ideas, which is the parent of all the harmonies among men. In order that any exchange between producer and consumer may come about, and still more, in order that any gift may be made to the consumer of the thing produced (for exchange is mutual giving, and as such is preceded by one-sided giving), the producer must first have experienced two notions simultaneously : that of a need on the part of the consumer or *donee*, and that of a means fitted to satisfy it. Without the internal adaptation of these two ideas, the external adaptation, first called gift and then exchange, would be impossible. Similarly, the division of labor

among a number of men, when they appor-
tion among themselves the different parts
of a single operation, hitherto executed
by one man, would not have been possible if the latter had not first conceived of
all these different works as parts of the
same whole, or means toward the same
end. At the basis of every association
among men, I repeat, there is originally
an association among the ideas of the
same man.

Let it not be objected that this adaptation of some ideas to others only deserves
to be called social when it expresses itself
in an adaptation of some men to others;
for it is often expressed otherwise, and
one might even say that the other manner
of expression tends to prevail. After the
labor of a single man has been replaced
in a certain case by a division of work
among several, it frequently happens that
a new invention causes all parts of the
operation to be performed by a single
machine. In this case, the division of

labor and the association of tasks among men plays merely the rôle of a middle term between the association of ideas in the mind of the first author of the production and the association of devices in the machine. Here the happy thought is not embodied in the group of workers, but materialized in the bits of iron or wood. And this sort of case tends to become more general with the improvements in the manufacture of machinery. Suppose, to take an impossible case, that all human productions were thus performed by machinery. There would be no more division of labor, since there would be no labor, or almost none, left; and we might even say that there was no real social *harmony* left; yet there would be a still greater degree of social *unity;* and this unity, which is far more desirable than that harmony, would be the result of a countless number of infinitely small cerebral adaptations. Where can we find any more powerful social factors than these phenomena, however individualistic they be?

We have just observed that the development of sociology, here as elsewhere, has brought it down from the dizzy heights of grand but vague causes, to real and precise acts of infinitesimal size. We have now to demonstrate, or rather point out (for there is no time for detailed examination), that the evolution of social facts, reversing the order of social science, consists in their gradual passage from a host of very small harmonies to a lesser number of greater ones, and then to a very small number of very great ones, till, in some indefinite future, the culmination of social progress is reached in a single, all-embracing civilization, which is also the most harmonious possible. It should be understood that this law of gradual enlargement is not here supposed to include the tendency of an invention or group of inventions to diffuse themselves by imitation;

this would be a return to the law of imitation with which we are already familiar. Nor, yet, is it concerned with the constant growth which this imitative radiation fosters in the social harmony which is called the division of labor, but which should more properly be called the solidarity of all labor. Supposing a certain industry to remain the same, with no further advances, the social cooperation that results therefrom will grow according as the needs of consumption to which it responds, on the one hand, and the acts of production by which it responds to them, on the other, are spread by imitation beyond the region, at first circumscribed, in which it originally appeared. However important may be the phenomenon of the growth of markets, which is the usual precursor of the federation of peoples, this is not here under discussion; indeed, it is unusual for this extrinsic growth to occur without some intrinsic industrial progress.

It is this intrinsic growth that we have
to discuss, that is, the tendency of a
given invention or social adaptation to
become larger and more complex by
adapting itself to some other invention
or adaptation, and thus create a new
adaptation, which, through other encounters and logical combinations of the same
sort, leads to a higher synthesis, and
so on. These two growths of invention
— its growth in *extension* by imitative
diffusion, and its growth in *comprehension*
by a series of logical combinations — are
certainly quite distinct, but, far from being mutually exclusive, and despite the
opposition between the extension and
comprehension of notions in other respects, they present a united front and
prove inseparable. Any mental association of two inventions that gives rise to a
third, — as, for instance, the notion of the
wheel and the notion of the domestica-
tion of the horse, which, after spreading
independently of one another for cen-

turies, perhaps, finally coalesced and har-
monized in the notion of the cart, — any
such association required necessarily the
function of imitation to bring the notions
together within the same mind, just as
previously, for the appearance of each,
its elements had to be brought to the
mind of its author by the radiation of
various examples. And, further, every
new synthesis of inventions requires,
generally, an imitative radiation of wider
scope than the preceding. There is
a constant interweaving of these two
growths: the unifying growth of imitation and the systematizing growth of
invention. The bond that binds them
together lacks universality, no doubt; for
a long succession of difficult theorems
may unroll themselves in the brain of
an Archimedes or a Newton, without the
aid of any elements contributed by other
scientists during the interval between
each two discoveries; yet it is so usual
a bond that we always expect to find

the extent of the social field, the completeness of social communications, and the breadth and depth of nationalities, as well as states, increasing *pari passu* with the wealth of languages, the architectural beauty of theologies, the cohesion of the sciences, the complexity and codification of laws, the spontaneous organization or legal supervision of industries, the system of finance, the complexity and coördination of government, and the refinements and varieties of literature and the fine arts.

Here, again, we must be careful not to confuse the *growth of education* (a mere phenomenon of imitation) with the *progress of science* (a phenomenon of adaptation), as is so often done ; nor the growth of industrialism with the progress of industry itself ; nor the growth of morality with the progress of ethics ; nor the growth of militarism with the progress of the military art ; nor yet the growth of a language, meaning thereby its territorial expansion, with the progress of that language, in the sense of increased refinement of its grammar and enrichment of its vocabulary. If science continues to progress while education ceases to spread further, the result is not the same as if education spread while science remained stationary, and we cannot combine the two cases by vaguely naming each an increase, or growth of illumination. On the contrary, they are two things that lack any common standard. Every gain of science, every truth added to her hoard, or *adaptate* of propositions that harmonize with one another, is not a mere summation, but rather a multiplication, and mutual confirmation; while every scholar added to the *aggregate*, every new brain copy added to the edition of taught science, is merely one unit more in the pile. To be exact, we must, of course, see in this something more than mere addition; for the community of intellect that results from the similarity of the education given to different children increases the confidence of each in his own knowledge,[1] and this also is a social adaptation, and not one of the least precious.

But before going further, we must pause to make a number of important observations. In the first place, let us note how much clearer and more exact the notion of adaptation becomes when we pass from the physical world, and even the world of life, to the social world. For, do we know precisely what constitutes the adaptation of an acid molecule to the basic molecule with which it combines? — or the adap-

---

[1] It should be noted in passing that this similarity of education is complete only in the primary schools, that it is less so in the secondary schools, in spite of the uniformity of requirements for the bachelor's degree, and that it is still less so in the higher schools or colleges, where a wide disagreement of teaching frequently appears. And the subordinate and mediate character of Contradiction and Discussion is revealed also in the fact that the higher education, where they flourish, always tends to degenerate into secondary education, where they are far less marked, and then into primary teaching, where they disappear entirely. The contradictions among scientists serve no purpose except to bring out certain adaptations of truths, for the future use of the rural schoolmaster.

tation of a grain of pollen to the ovule which, after being fertilized by it, gives birth to a new individual, the founder, perhaps, of a new race? We certainly do not know anything definite about it. It is true that, when two sound-waves interfere, and instead of destroying each other, are of mutual assistance, so that they produce a reënforcement of the sound or some unexpected timbre effect, we understand somewhat better the nature of the phenomenon; but, as a matter of fact, this mere reënforcement of the sound or production of a new timbre is an original creation only from the standpoint of our subjective sensations of hearing, and has nothing in common with the objective innovation resulting from chemical combination. Similarly, when two animal or vegetable species come together in such a way that each serves as the other's aid or parasite, this clear case of mutual assistance among living things gives rise simply to an increase of their well-being and number, and must not be confounded with the phenomenon of fertilization, which remains extremely obscure. But, when a felicitous interference occurs between two imitative radiations, whatever its nature, our reason can always grasp its meaning. It may consist merely in a mutual stimulation, as when the increased use of the Auer gas-jet favored an increased use of gas, or when the wider diffusion of the French language favored a wider diffusion of French literature, which in turn favored the spread of the former. It may also happen that this interference proves of great efficacy and gives rise to some new invention, a centre from which new rays of imitation start; thus the use of copper, encountering one day the use of tin, suggested the idea of making bronze; and so, too, the knowledge of algebra and geometry suggested to Descartes the algebraic expression of curves. But in the latter case, as in the former, we see clearly that adaptation is either a logical

N

or a teleological relation, and that it can always be referred to one or other of these two types; sometimes, as in the case of Newton's Law, or any scientific law whatsoever, it is a synthesis of ideas which formerly seemed neither to confirm nor to contradict one another, and which now prove to be mutually confirmatory, as consequences of the same principle; or, again, as in the case of some industrial machine, it is a synthesis of acts which were formerly strangers to one another, and now, being brought together in some ingenious way, serve as common means to a single end. The invention of the cart (itself a complex affair, as we know), the discovery of iron, the discovery of the motive power of steam, the invention of the piston, and the invention of the rail, — all these inventions, which once seemed foreign to one another, have been brought together in the invention of the locomotive.

In the second place, whether we take a synthesis of acts, or some invention, —

industrial or scientific, religious or æsthetic, — in short, whether we are dealing
with the theoretical or the practical, the
fundamental process that enters into its
make-up is always what may be called
logical association by pairs; for, whatever be the number of notions or actions
that a theory or a machine synthesizes,
there are never more than two elements
combined at a time, and adapted to one
another, in the mind of the inventor, or
any of the inventors that assisted, in turn,
in its production.[1]   In his recent work on
Semantic, M. Bréal, speaking of language,
makes an acute observation, which lends
support to this general principle : " Whatever be the length of a compound word,"
he says, " it never includes more than two
terms.   This is no arbitrary rule ; it comes
from the nature of our intellect, which

[1] See, in my *Laws of Imitation*, the chapter on the
Logical Laws of Imitation, especially p. 175 and p. 195 f.
(French edition) ; and in my *Social Logic*, the chapter
on the *Laws of Invention*.

always associates its notions in pairs."
In another passage, referring to the
schematic figures by means of which
James Darmesteter endeavors to make
clear to the eye the development of the
significance of words through various
channels, the same author says: "We
must remember that these complex figures have no value, except for a single
linguist; for, whoever invents a new
meaning for a word, forgets, for the time
being, all its previous meanings except
one, so that associations of ideas always
occur in pairs." And in this they corre-
spond to oppositions of ideas, as we have
observed. It would be easy, though of
course it would take too long, to show
how general this process really is, by examining in turn the manner in which each
discovery or improvement was added to
some previous discovery, whether in the
scientific, legal, economic, political, artistic,
or moral spheres. Rather, let us indicate
here why it is so, that is, how the phe-

nomenon is rendered possible and necessary.

It is due chiefly to this. On the one hand, the course of the mind's activity, its fundamental procedure, consists in passing from one idea to another, and uniting the two by means of a judgment or volition — a judgment which exhibits the idea of the attribute as implicated in that of the subject, or a volition which regards the idea of the means as implicated in that of the end. On the other hand, when the mind passes from some judgment to another which is more complex, or from some volition to another which is more comprehensive, it is because, by dint of mental repetition in that dual form of self-imitation called memory or habit, a judgment is compressed into a notion, so that its two terms, coalescing, are welded together and become indistinguishable, and a volition or aim is transformed into a reflex involving ever less of consciousness. By this inevitable transformation, which operates socially on a large scale, under the revered titles of tradition and custom, our former judgments are fitted to enter, under the guise of notions, into the substance of some new judgment, and our former aims into the substance of some new aim. From the lowest to the highest operation of our understanding and will, this process occurs unaltered. No theoretical discovery is anything but the union, in a judgment, of an attribute (that is, of earlier judgments) with some new subject; and, similarly, no practical discovery is other than the voluntary union of a means (that is, an end formerly desired for its own sake) with a new end. Thus by an alternation, at once most simple and most fruitful, of contrary transformations which succeed one another *ad infinitum*, yesterday's judgment or end becomes simply to-day's notion or means, and will pass over into to-morrow's judgment or end, which is destined, in turn, to succumb to the same process of consolidation, and so on. Through this rhythm, which is at once social and psychological, there have gradually been raised the many grand structures of accumulated discoveries and inventions that so excite our admiration : our languages, religions, sciences, codes, and administrative systems, as well as our military organization, industries, and arts.

When we consider one of the greater social phenomena, such as a grammar, a code, or a theology, the individual mind appears so trivial a thing beside these monumental works that the idea of regarding it as the sole artisan concerned in the erection of these enormous cathedrals seems to some sociologists quite absurd ; and one may readily be excused if, without perceiving that he thereby abandons all attempt at explanation, he is drawn into saying that these works are eminently impersonal; yet there is but a step from this position to that of my illustrious opponent, M. Durkheim, who insists that they are not *functions* of the individual, but his *factors*, and that they have an existence independent of human personality, and rule man with despotic might, by the oppressive shadow which they cast over him. But how have these social realities come into being? (I say *realities*, for, although I oppose the idea of a social organism, I am far from challenging the concept of certain social realities, concerning which some understanding must be reached.) I see clearly that, once formed, they impose themselves upon the individual, sometimes, though rarely, with constraint, oftener by persuasion or suggestion or the curious pleasure that we experience, from childhood up, in saturating ourselves with the examples of our myriad surrounding models, as the babe in imbibing its mother's milk. This I see clearly enough; but how were these wonderful monuments constructed, and by whom, if not by men and through human efforts?

As regards the structure of science, probably the most imposing of human edifices, there is no possible question. It was built in the full light of history, and we can follow its development almost from the very outset down to our own day. Our sciences began as a scattered and disconnected collection of small discoveries, which were afterward grouped into little theories (each group being itself a discovery); and the latter were welded, later, into broader theories, to be confirmed or amended by a host of other discoveries, and finally bound firmly together by the arches of hypotheses built over them by the spirit of unification: this manner of progress is indisputable. There is no law nor scientific theory (any more than there is a system of philosophy) that does not bear its author's name still legibly written. Everything here originates in the individual; not only the materials, but the general design of the whole, and the detail sketches as well; everything, including what is now diffused among all cultured minds, and taught even in the primary school, began as the secret of some single mind, whence a little flame, faint and flickering, sent forth its rays, at first only within a narrow compass, and even there encountering many obstructions, but, growing brighter as it spread further, it at length became a brilliant illumination.

Now, if it seems plainly evident that science was thus constructed, it is no less true that the construction of every dogma, legal code, government, or economic *régime* was effected in the same manner; and if any doubt be possible with respect to language and ethics, because the obscurity of their origin and the slowness of their transformations remove them from observation through the greater part of their course, is it not highly probable that their evolution followed the same path? For, it is by minute accretions of image-laden expressions, picturesque phrases, and new words, or words new in

meaning, that our language enriches itself to-day ; and, though each of these innovations is usually unsigned, it is none
the less due to some personal initiative,
imitated by first one and then another ; and
these happy expressions which swarm in
every language are just what different languages, brought into mutual relation, are
continually borrowing from one another,
to enlarge their vocabulary, and render
their grammar more flexible, and at the
same time more complicated. So, too, it
is through a series of petty, individual
revolts against the accepted ethics, or
through petty, individual additions to its
precepts, that this system of ethics undergoes a gradual modification. Thus we
have advanced by successive stages, from
a remote era, when languages were countless in number, but poverty-stricken, and
each spoken by a single populace, tribe, or
town, and when ethical codes were very
numerous, dissimilar, and simple, to an
epoch when a small number of very

wealthy languages, and very complex codes of morality, contend for future supremacy on the earth.

One thing, however, must be granted to the opponents of the theory of individual causes in history; namely, that writers have frequently made the mistake of speaking of great men when they should have spoken of great ideas, which often appear in very unimportant men, or of the trivial ideas and infinitesimal innovations contributed by each of us to the common work. For, as a matter of fact, all, or nearly all of us, have had a share in the building of these enormous structures that overshadow and protect us; each one of us, however orthodox he be, has his own religion, and each, however precise, his own language and ethics; the most commonplace of scientists has his own science, and the most bureaucratic of officials his own system of administration. And just as each, consciously or unconsciously, adds his own little invention to the enduring heritage of social material of which he is the temporary repository, so, too, each has his own imitative radiation in a sphere more or less contracted, which, nevertheless, suffices to prolong his discovery beyond his own ephemeral existence and pass it on to future workmen who may make some definite use of it. Imitation, which socializes the individual, also perpetuates good ideas from every source, and in the process of perpetuating them brings them together and makes them fertile.

It may possibly be urged, then, that, given the eternal nature of things, in conjunction with the human mind, itself an enduring object, human science was bound inevitably to reach, sooner or later, by it matters not what path of individual discovery, the stage in which we now see it, and the stage in which our grandchildren will see it; that its future form, bright and glorious, was already predetermined from the earliest perceptions of the sav-

age ; and, hence, that the rôle of the individual and the brilliant accident of genius
are of slight importance, or lose their importance every day, as we approach that
ideal reality, of Platonic attractiveness,
whose outline we are now beginning to
discern. But such an objection, if true,
must be generalized, and it would then
follow that some irresistible attraction,
divinely planned and invisible, must be
driving all humanity onward, by a certain chain of satisfactions and needs, born
successively of one another, to the same
final political goal, whether economic or
otherwise, and to the same constitution,
industrial system, language, and legislation. Hitherto this view has proved most
contrary to fact; for, the more the different civilizations — Christian, Buddhistic, or
Mohammedan — which divide the earth
between them have developed, the more
marked have become their distinctions and
dissimilarities. What pleases me especially
in this theory is its idealism ; but it is

not sufficiently idealistic, and hence mis-
represents that view. For it is not a single idea, nor a small number of ideas,
hovering in mid-air, that move the world ;
rather, there are thousands upon thousands
striving for the distinction of having led
it. The ideas that stir up the world are
the ideas of the actors upon its stage, each
one of whom has fought to effect the triumph of his own ideas in some dream of
local, national, or international reconstruc-
tion, which developed as it realized itself,
and sometimes grew bolder even after it
was vanquished. Each character in history is the model of a new humanity, and
his entire personality and individual efforts
are but the expression of that incipient
universal which he bears within himself.
And of these countless ideas, these great
patriotic or humanitarian projects, that
wave above the struggling mass of humanity like great banners mutually rent
asunder, one alone, possibly, out of myri-
ads, is destined to survive ; but even this

must have been personal in origin, bursting forth, some time, from the head or heart of some man. I am willing to grant that this triumph was necessary; but its *necessity*, which appeared afterward, and which no one saw in advance, or could have foreseen with certainty, is merely a verbal expression for the superiority of the individual efforts enlisted in support of this particular conception. Final cause and efficient causes are mingled here, and there is no good reason for distinguishing them.

It is because the material and plans of every social construction are all individual contributions, that I am unwilling to admit the despotic and resistless nature of the constraint placed upon the individual, which has been considered the essential and distinctive characteristic of social phenomena. Were this the case, the sphere of truth could never grow, and these structures could never have been built; for, in each of the suc-

cessive steps of growth through the addition of some innovation (such as a
new word, proposed law, scientific theory, industrial process, etc.), the new-
comer obtains admittance, not by force,
but by gentle persuasion and suggestion.
Observe the manner in which the pala-
tial edifice of science has grown. Some
theory is long discussed in the sphere
of higher learning, before it spreads in
the form of a more or less probable hypothesis, and at length descends into the
sphere of secondary education, where it
is more rigorously accepted; but, generally, it is only after such a theory reaches
the sphere of primary education that it
becomes quite dogmatic, and exerts, or
endeavors to exert, the far from despotic
coercion already referred to on the minds
of its youthful adherents, who lend themselves to this coercion with the greatest
willingness. This means, in other words,
that its present imperative character has
arisen by virtue of its former persuasive-

o

ness, and the whole through imitative diffusion. The same holds true of any industrial innovation that spreads; it is the caprice of a chosen few before it becomes a public need and forms part of the necessities of life. For the luxuries of to-day are the necessities of to-morrow, in the same way that the higher education of to-day becomes the secondary or primary instruction of to-morrow.

This great problem of social adaptation ought really to be traced out along numerous other lines; some of these I have sketched in my work on *Social Logic*, to which I may refer here. But we must set a limit somewhere. I need scarcely insist upon the fact, unfortunately only too plain, that, as these adaptations multiply and become more definite, at the same time certain distressing and perplexing social *inadaptations* come to light, which justify so many of man's complaints. However, we are now in a better position to explain why the natural

harmonies, as well as the natural symmetries, are rarely perfect, and why we
find accompanying them and mixed up
with them certain disharmonies and dissymmetries which sometimes contribute
to the production of higher adaptations
and oppositions. It is because perfect
adaptation and perfect opposition are but
the two limits of an infinite series, between which are countless intermediary
positions. Between the absolute confirmation of one proposition by another, and
an absolute contradiction between the
two, there are an infinite number of partial contradictions and partial confirma-
tions, without counting the infinite number
of degrees of affirmative and negative
belief. Invention is a question followed
by an answer. But for each question
set a thousand answers are possible, of
all possible degrees of completeness and
exactness. To the question concerning
the need of sight, not merely has the
human eye responded, but throughout na-

ture there are all the various eyes of insects, birds, and molluscs. And, similarly, to the question concerning the need of recording speech, the Phœnician alphabet was not the only one to respond.

At the basis of every society we find a host of answers, both great and small, to the various questions proposed, and a host of new questions arising out of these very answers; and it is for this reason that we find also a large number of struggles, great or small, between the advocates of various solutions. Strife is merely a coming together of harmonies; but this kind of encounter is not the only relation that exists between harmonies; their most common relation is agreement — the production of a superior harmony. Every moment, whether we are speaking or working at any task whatsoever, we both feel a need and satisfy it; and it is these series of satisfactions or solutions, that make up con-

versation and labor, as well as domestic
and international politics, diplomacy, and
war,—in short, all forms of human activity. The constantly renewed efforts
of the individuals in a nation to adapt
their language to their passing thoughts[1]
are what cause the gradual modification
and transformation of speech, and the
birth of new languages. If a record
could have been kept, as Abbé Rousselot endeavored to do in a small sec-
tion of Charente, of all these successive
efforts, we would be able to note the
exact number of *fundamental linguistic
adaptations* that have been integrated
into a modification of the sound or sense
of words. Similarly, all men, but especially those who feel that they are most
ill-adapted to their environment and to
themselves, are constantly endeavoring to
adapt their dogmas and religious precepts to their needs and knowledge, and
to adapt their customs and laws and

[1] On this subject see M. Bréal's *Semantic.*

even their moral code to the same;
and these constant efforts result in a
gradual accumulation of slight improvements.[1] Then, too, from time to time,

---

[1] If we wish to make sociology a truly experimental
science and stamp it with the seal of absolute exactness, we must, I believe, generalize the method of Abbé
Rousselot in its essential features, through the collaboration of a great number of trustworthy observers. Let
twenty, thirty, or as many as fifty sociologists, from
different sections of France or any other country, write
out with the greatest care and in the greatest possible
detail the succession of minute transformations in the
political or industrial world, or some other sphere of
life, which it is their privilege to observe in their native
town or village, beginning with their own immediate
surroundings. Instead of limiting themselves to vague
generalities, let them note in full the specific instances
of the rise or fall of religious or political faith, of morality or immorality, of luxury, comfort, and whatever
modifications of political or religious belief have occurred
under their eyes since they reached the age of reason,
beginning with their own family and circle of friends.
Let them strive to the utmost, like the noted linguist
already mentioned, to trace out the individual sources
of the slight diminutions, augmentations, or transformations of ideas and tendencies which have spread through
a certain group of men, and which are expressed by
imperceptible changes in language, gesture, toilet, and
other customs. Let this be done, and within such a

some great inventor or some great har-
monizer arises.

Disharmonies are to harmonies what
dissymmetries are to symmetries and va-

highly instructive body of monographs there cannot
fail to appear certain most important truths — truths
most valuable for the sociologist and statesman to know.
These *narrative* monographs would differ radically from
our present *descriptive* monographs, and would be far
more enlightening. To understand social *conditions*, we
must seize social *changes* in detail as they pass; while
the converse is not true. For, however much we ac-
cumulate instances of the concurrence of social conditions in every country of the world, the law of their
formation does not appear, or rather, it is covered up
by the mass of collected evidence. But any one who
knew thoroughly, in exact detail, the changes of custom
on some particular points, in a single country and
during ten years, could not fail to lay his hand upon
a general principle of social transformation, and consequently upon a principle of social *formation*, that
would apply to every land and to all time. In such a
research it would be well to take up a very limited
number of questions : for instance, it might first be
asked, by whom and how the custom was originally introduced and generalized, among the peasants of certain
rural districts in southern France, of not saluting
the well-to-do proprietors of their neighborhood ; or
through what influences the belief in sorcery, the
were-wolf, and the like, begin to disappear.

riations to repetitions. It is from the midst of exact repetitions, absolute contrasts, and perfect harmonies, that the best examples of general diversity, picturesqueness, and disorder appear, namely, the individual characteristics of things. The expression of a man or woman's face, refined by the influences of the social life and the intense, complex, and ceaseless life of imitation, is a small and fleeting phenomenon. Yet there is nothing so important as just this fugitive shade of expression. And no painter has succeeded in catching it; no poet or novelist has recalled it to life, no matter how hard he has striven in the attempt. The thinker has no right to smile at sight of their long-continued endeavors to grasp this almost tangible thing, which never has been, and never can be, recalled. There is no *science* of the individual, but *art* is wholly of the individual. And the scientist, remembering that the life of the universe depends entirely on the fruition of personal individuality, would be compelled to reflect on the artist's labor with a humility mingled with some envy, did he not himself, by stamping his personal seal on his own general notion of phenomena, always impart to that notion an æsthetic value, the real *raison d'être* of his thought.

CONCLUSION

IT is now time to conclude; but, in concluding, let us sum up the principal positions to which we have been led, and seek to understand the meaning of their conjunction. We observed that all science subsisted on similarities, contrasts (or symmetries), and harmonies, that is, on repetitions, oppositions, and adaptations; and we asked what was the law of each of these three terms, as well as their relation with one another. We have seen that, in spite of its natural and *a priori* apparently legitimate tendency to choose the greatest, most widespread, and most imposing phenomena to explain the less marked, the human mind has been irresistibly led to discover the underlying principle of every order of things in the most hidden facts, whose depths, it is true, remain unsounded. This discovery ought to cause great surprise; yet it does nothing of the sort, for the habit of scientific observation has made us thoroughly familiar with such reversals of the order imagined by our earlier thought. Thus the law of repetition, whether we mean by this the undulatory and rotatory repetition of the physical world, the hereditary and habit-like repetition of the world of life, or the imitative repetition of the social world, implies a tendency to move along a path of steady growth, from a comparatively infinitesimal to a comparatively infinite scale. The law of opposition is in no way different; it consists in a tendency to enlarge in an ever widening sphere, beginning with a certain point in the world of life; this point is the brain of some individual, and more specifically a cell in this brain, where a contradiction

between two beliefs or two desires is produced by an interference between imitative rays from without. Such is the
fundamental social opposition, which is
the moving principle of the bloodiest
wars, in the same way that the fundamental social repetition is the specific
fact of the existence of some first imita-
tor, who forms the starting-point of a great
epidemic of custom. Finally, the law
of adaptation is similar; the fundamental
social adaptation is some individual invention that is destined to be imitated, that
is, the felicitous interference of two imitations, occurring first in one single mind;
and this harmony, though quite internal
in origin, tends not only to externalize
itself as it spreads, but also to unite
with some other invention, in a logical
couple, thanks to this imitative diffusion,
and so on, until, by successive complica-
tions and harmonizations of the harmonies, the grand collective works of the
human mind are constructed, — a gram-

mar, a theology, an encyclopædia, a code
of laws, a natural or artificial organization of labor, a scheme of æsthetics or
a system of ethics.

Thus, in a word, everything undoubtedly
starts with the infinitely minute ; and we
may add that it probably returns thither ;
this is its alpha and omega. Everything
that constitutes the visible universe, the
universe accessible to observation, proceeds, as we know, out of the invisible and
inscrutable, — out of a seeming nothing-
ness, — whence all reality emerges in an
inexhaustible stream. If we reflect on
this curious phenomenon, we shall be astonished at the strength of the prejudice,
both popular and scientific, which makes
every one, whether he be a Spencer or
the first man we chance to meet, regard
the infinitesimal as insignificant, that is, as
homogeneous, neutral, and possessed of
neither soul nor individuality. How per-
sistent an illusion this is ! And it is all
the more inexplicable because, like every-

thing else, we, too, are destined soon to return, through death, to this despised infinitesimal from whence we are sprung — which may be (who knows?) the real *beyond*, that haven in the hereafter, so vainly sought for amid the infinities of space. However this may be, what reason have we for concluding *a priori*, without a knowledge of the world of elements, that the visible world, the great world about us, is the sole scene of thought and seat of the various phenomena of life? How can we imagine such a thing, when every moment we see some personal being, with peculiar and radiating characteristics, springing forth from the inmost recesses of a fertilized egg and from the inmost recesses of a certain part of that egg — a part that grows constantly smaller, almost to the vanishing point, in proportion as we get a better view of it? Can we imagine this limiting point, the source of such important differences, to be itself undifferentiated?

I am aware of the objection that will be raised in the supposed law of the instability of the homogeneous. But this law is false and arbitrary; it was conceived merely for the sake of reconciling the notion that what is indistinguishable to our eyes is really undifferentiated, with the evidences of diversity among phenomena and the exuberant variations that appear in the organic, psychological, and social spheres. The truth is that only the heterogeneous is unstable, while the homogeneous is essentially stable. The stability of phenomena varies directly with their homogeneity. The only perfectly homogeneous thing (or apparently so) in nature is the space of geometry, which has not altered since Euclid. Will it be maintained that some very minute germ of heterogeneity, introduced into a relatively homogeneous aggregate, like yeast in a cake, is bound to bring about a growing differentiation? This I dispute; for in an orthodox land, where religious or politi-

cal opinions all agree, a heresy or dissent-
ing view that is introduced has far more
chance of being absorbed or expelled in
short order than of growing at the expense
of the dominant church or political party.
I do not deny the law of differentiation
in its organic or social bearings; but it is
sadly misunderstood if it prevents us from
seeing the *law of increasing unification* that
mingles with it and coöperates with it. In
reality, the differentiation in question is
the very adaptation that we have been discussing : thus, for instance, the division of
labor in our social organizations is merely
a gradual association or coadaptation of
different labors by means of successive
inventions. Confined to the *household*
first of all, it proceeded to repeat and
enlarge itself unceasingly. It extended
itself first to the city, where various house-
holds, formerly similar to one another,
though each differentiated within itself,
became more unlike one another, though
each more homogeneous in itself. Later

on, it became national, and at length international.

It is not true, then, that differences increase in number; for, if new differences appear every instant, old differences vanish at the same time; and taking this into consideration, we have no reason for supposing that the sum total of differences (if, indeed, it be possible to add together things which have no element in common) has really increased in the universe. But something far more important than a mere increase of difference is constantly taking place, namely, the differentiation of the differences themselves. The process of change is itself undergoing a change, in a direction that is taking us from an era of the crudest juxtaposition of differences, such as startling and unblended colors, to an era of harmoniously shaded differences. Whatever may be thought of this particular view, it is nevertheless inconceivable, upon the hypothesis of a homogeneous

P

substance subject from eternity to the levelling and coördinating influences of scientific laws, how a universe such as ours, luxuriating in surprises and caprice, could ever have come into existence. What can spring from a perfectly similar and perfectly coördinated system, except a world eternally and superlatively uniform? And so, in place of the usual conception of the universe as being formed (like an enormous sand-heap) of elements quite similar at bottom, whence diversity sprang in some unaccountable manner, I propose this conception of my own, which represents it as the realization of a host of elementary potentialities,[1] each possessing individuality and ambition, and containing in itself its own distinctive universe, the object of its dreams. For an infinitely greater number of fundamental projects miscarry

[1] On this subject see the study entitled *Monadology and Sociology*, in my *Essais et Mélanges* (Paris and Lyons, Storck & Masson, 1895).

than ever reach full development; and
the great struggle for existence, through
which the least adapted beings are eliminated, is waged between competing dreams
and rival projects, rather than different
beings. Thus the mysterious basement
of the phenomenal world may be quite
as rich in differences, though differences
of another sort, as the upper stories of
visible, superficial realities.

Yet, after all, the metaphysical theory
that I have just indicated is of slight
importance in comparison with the *exposé*
that precedes it, and I merely put forward this hypothesis in parenthesis, with
the remark that, even if it be rejected,
the more solid and more positive arguments presented above still remain stand-
ing. It merely permits us to gather
within a single heading the two apparently different kinds of fact that we have
met with in the course of our journey :
namely, the facts pertaining to the regular succession of repetitions, struggles,

and harmonies in the universe, — in other words, the regular side of the universe, which is the subject-matter of science, — and those relating to the more uncouth aspect of the universe, which art delights continually to seize and reproduce, and which satisfy (as it would seem) an eternal craving for diversity, picturesqueness, and disorder, through the operation of this same universal assimilation, symmetrization, and harmonization. It is the easiest thing in the world to understand this apparent anomaly, if we grant that the sub-phenomenal differences of things are forever striving, not to efface themselves, but to blossom out and appear at the surface. Then, everything is explained. The mutual relations of our three terms — repetition, opposition, and adaptation — are easily understood, when we consider successive repetitions as operating sometimes in favor of adaptation, which they spread and develop by their own interferences, sometimes in favor of

opposition, which they arouse by interferences of another sort. And, similarly,
we may believe that all three of these
factors work together to effect the ex-
pansion of universal variation in its highest, widest, and profoundest individual
and personal forms.

OCTOBER, 1897.

PERSPECTIVES IN SOCIAL INQUIRY

CLASSICS, STAPLES AND PRECURSORS IN SOCIOLOGY

Authority and the Individual. 1937

Baldwin, James Mark. **The Individual and Society:** Or,Psychology and Sociology. 1911

Beaglehole, Ernest. **Property:** A Study in Social Psychology. 1932

Beard, Charles A. **The Nature of the Social Sciences:** In Relation to Objectives of Instruction. 1934

Burrow, Trigant. **The Biology of Human Conflict:** An Anatomy of Behavior, Individual and Social. 1937

Carr-Saunders, A. M. **The Population Problem:** A Study in Human Evolution. 1922

Carver, Thomas Nixon. **The Essential Factors of Social Evolution.** 1935

Congress of Arts and Science: Selected Papers. 1906

De Man, Henry. **The Psychology of Socialism.** [1928]

Factors Determining Human Behavior. 1937

Giddings, Franklin Henry. **The Scientific Study of Human Society.** 1924

Hayward, F[rank] H. **Professionalism and Originality.** 1917

Huntington, Ellsworth. **World-Power and Evolution.** 1920

Hurry, Jamieson B. **Poverty and Its Vicious Circles.** 1917

Jenks, Edward. **The State and The Nation.** 1919

Judd, Charles Hubbard. **The Psychology of Social Institutions.** 1927

Kelsen, Hans. **Society and Nature:** A Sociological Inquiry. 1946

Lange, Frederick Albert. **The History of Materialism:** And Criticism of Its Present Importance. 3 vols. in 1. 1879-1881

Le Bon, Gustave. **The Psychology of Peoples.** 1924

Lewis, George Cornewall. **An Essay on the Influence of Authority in Matters of Opinion.** 1849

Lewis, George Cornewall. **A Treatise on the Methods of Observation and Reasoning in Politics.** 2 vols. in 1. 1852

Lowell, Abbot Lawrence. **Public Opinion in War and Peace.** 1923

Maine, Henry Sumner. **Village-Communities in the East and West.** 1889

Merton, Robert K. and Paul F. Lazarsfeld, eds. **Continuities in Social Research:** Studies in the Scope and Method of "The American Soldier." 1950

Michels, Roberto. **First Lectures in Political Sociology.** 1949

Ogburn, William Fielding and Alexander Goldenweiser, eds. **The Social Sciences and Their Interrelations.** 1927

Park, Robert Ezra. **The Collected Papers of Robert Ezra Park.** 3 vols. in 1. 1950/52/55

Plint, Thomas. **Crime in England:** Its Relation, Character and Extent as Developed from 1801 to 1848. 1851

Ranulf, Svend. **The Jealousy of the Gods and Criminal Law at Athens.** 2 vols. in 1. 1933/34

Ross, Edward Alsworth. **Social Psychology:** An Outline and Source Book. 1912

Small, Albion W. **General Sociology.** 1905

Studies in Social Psychology in World War II: Vols. I, II, and III. 1949

Sutherland, Alexander. **The Origin and Growth of the Moral Instinct.** 2 vols. in 1. 1898

Tarde, G[abriel]. **Social Laws:** An Outline of Sociology. 1899

Teggart, Frederick J. **Prolegomena to History.** 1916

Thomas, William I. **Sex and Society.** 1907

Von Wiese, Leopold. **Systematic Sociology.** 1932

Ward, Lester F. **Applied Sociology.** 1906

Wirth, Louis, ed. **Eleven Twenty-Six:** A Decade of Social Science Research. 1940

Wright, R[obert] J[oseph]. **Principia, Or Basis of Social Science.** 1875